Pupil Book 6A

Series Editor: Peter Clarke

Authors: Elizabeth Jurgensen, Jeanette Mumford, Sandra Roberts

Contents

7-digit numbers

Read and write numbers to 10 000 000 and determine the value of each digit

Challenge 1

1 Write the place value of each digit in these numbers.

Example
185 386 = 100 000 + 80 000 + 5000 + 300 + 80 + 6

a 367 912   b 205 936   c 617 483

d 558 165   e 926 815   f 783 402

g 833 639   h 970 275   i 862 206

2 Choose four of the numbers from Question 1 and write them out in words.

Challenge 2

1 Write the place value of each digit in these numbers.

Example
3 753 193 = 3 000 000 + 700 000 + 50 000 + 3000 + 100 + 90 + 3

a 4 872 128   b 1 631 197   c 5 502 472   d 2 378 207

e 7 927 802   f 5 047 155   g 7 825 831   h 9 777 222

2 Choose four of the numbers from Question 1 and write them out in words.

3 Each of these cards represents the place value of a digit in a number.
Make ten 7-digit numbers using these cards.

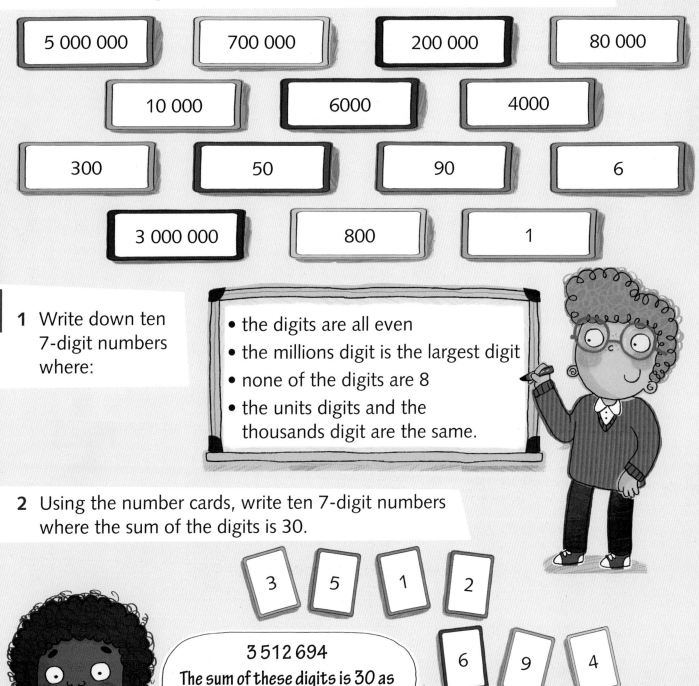

| 5 000 000 | 700 000 | 200 000 | 80 000 |

| 10 000 | 6000 | 4000 |

| 300 | 50 | 90 | 6 |

| 3 000 000 | 800 | 1 |

1 Write down ten 7-digit numbers where:

- the digits are all even
- the millions digit is the largest digit
- none of the digits are 8
- the units digits and the thousands digit are the same.

2 Using the number cards, write ten 7-digit numbers where the sum of the digits is 30.

3 5 1 2   6 9 4

3 512 694
The sum of these digits is 30 as
3 + 5 + 1 + 2 + 6 + 9 + 4 = 30

3 Using the numbers you made in Question 2, play this game with a partner.

You will need:
- 0–9 dice

- Take turns to say a place value, for example, millions.
- Roll the dice. If you have that digit in the chosen place value, cross it out.
- The first player to cross out one whole number is the winner.

7-digit ordering

Order and compare numbers to 10 000 000 and determine the value of each digit

1 Order each set of numbers, smallest to largest.

a 487 397, 419 386, 463 297, 402 392, 453 927

b 783 297, 719 235, 773 227, 785 297, 760 383

c 279 385, 234 297, 285 268, 271 297, 237 251

d 659 286, 651 375, 658 295, 650 286, 658 296

e 305 286, 305 816, 305 047, 305 575, 305 773

f 596 287, 591 486, 562 286, 594 386, 561 386

g 837 393, 839 486, 837 083, 839 382, 837 187

h 993 365, 996 262, 993 261, 996 100, 993 325

i 324 751, 340 794, 315 888, 348 546, 312 135

j 96 104, 161 171, 107 356, 150 281, 137 790

Hint
Always compare digits with the highest place value first.

2 Write the next number.

a 562 349

b 403 499

c 608 369

d 199 999

e 725 439

f 640 589

g 714 329

h 268 009

i 692 449

j 511 479

1 Copy out these numbers and write a number in the spaces, still keeping the order.

a	2 398 363,	2 408 826,	2 489 275,	,	, 2 496 887
b	5 400 250,	5 400 650,	5 400 850,	,	, 5 400 999
c	7 654 000,	7 655 000,	7 656 000,	,	, 7 676 000
d	3 154 782,	3 583 773,	3 591 375,	,	, 3 592 406
e	6 247 222,	6 248 022,	6 248 200,	,	, 6 249 582
f	9 736 187,	9 745 376,	9 750 075,	,	, 9 755 010
g	4 000 000,	5 000 000,	6 000 000,	,	, 9 000 000
h	8 408 383,	8 523 374,	8 583 750,	,	, 8 583 820
i	7 401 916,	7 651 898,	7 822 620,	,	, 7 822 630
j	1 878 096,	1 878 596,	1 878 637,	,	, 1 878 642

2 Write the next number.

a	5 478 300	**b**	1 208 269	**c**	4 832 297
d	8 289 599	**e**	4 295 000	**f**	3 199 999
g	8 497 209	**h**	2 638 890	**i**	3 432 729
j	5 299 305	**k**	7 684 319	**l**	9 999 999

1 Use the number cards to make ten different 7-digit numbers.

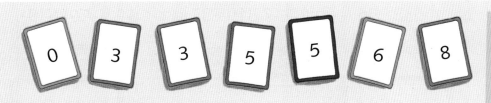

2 Order your numbers, smallest to largest.

3 Explain how to order 7-digit numbers.

Hint
Organising your numbers in a systematic way will help you to check that you do not repeat any answers.

Rounding 7-digit numbers

Round any whole number to a required degree of accuracy

Challenge 1

1 Write the multiples of 10, 100 and 1000 that each number comes between.

Example

147 360 ← 147 362 → 147 370
147 300 ← 147 362 → 147 400
147 000 ← 147 362 → 148 000

a 265 892   b 487 371   c 306 385

d 725 247   e 846 794   f 532 766

g 921 653   h 798 518   i 642 386

2 For each of your answers in Question 1, circle the multiple that the number rounds to.

Challenge 2

1 Write the multiples of 10, 100 and 1000 that each number comes between.

a 3 973 729   b 4 538 255   c 7 315 837   d 5 724 619

e 6 838 711   f 8 526 584   g 4 652 176   h 6 237 453

2 For each of your answers in Question 1, circle the multiple that the number rounds to.

3 For each of the numbers below, write three numbers that, when rounded down, equal the number. In brackets beside your numbers show the degree of rounding.

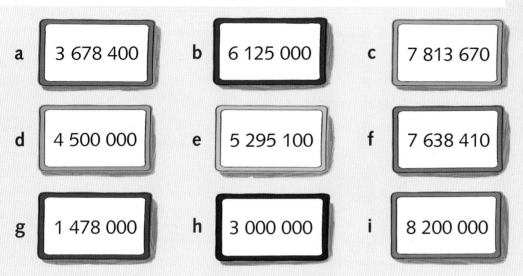

Example

5 684 700

5 684 701 (10)
5 684 720 (100)
5 684 740 (100)

a 3 678 400   b 6 125 000   c 7 813 670

d 4 500 000   e 5 295 100   f 7 638 410

g 1 478 000   h 3 000 000   i 8 200 000

1 Write the multiples of 10 000, 100 000 and 1 000 000 that each number comes between.

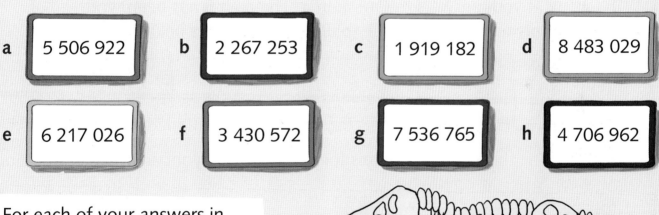

a 5 506 922   b 2 267 253   c 1 919 182   d 8 483 029

e 6 217 026   f 3 430 572   g 7 536 765   h 4 706 962

2 For each of your answers in Question 1, circle the multiple that the number rounds to.

T-Rex

3 In one year, a museum had 4 691 692 visitors and 1456 complaints.

Write a report on behalf of the museum explaining these figures. Make sure that your report is worded in a way that looks best for the museum. You may want to round these numbers to different degrees.

Now write a statement explaining why you included these numbers in your report.

Changing digits

Solve number problems

Challenge 1

This 6-digit number is standing at the bus stop:

If the first digit goes to the back of the queue, the new number will be:

a   Copy the two numbers above. Imagine that the digits keep going to the back of the queue, one by one. Write the other four new numbers they will make.

b   Look at your answers to Question **a**. The digit 5 has been worth all of the amounts below. What is the total of all the values below?

| 500 000 | 5 | 50 | 500 | 5 000 | 50 000 |

c   Write all the values and totals for these digits in your answers to Question **a**.
   i 8   ii 2   iii 7

d   Explain the reason the totals are made up of the same digit.

Challenge 2

This 7-digit number is standing at the bus stop:

If the first digit goes to the back of the queue, the new number will be:

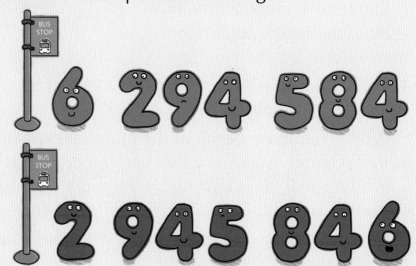

a Copy the two numbers. Imagine that the digits keep going to the back of the queue, one by one. Write the other five new numbers they will make.

b Look at your answers to Question **a**. The digit 6 has been worth different amounts.

    i Write down all the different values.

    ii What is the total of all the values?

c Write all the values and totals for these digits in your answers to Question **a**.

    i 9   **ii** 5   **iii** 8

d Explain the reason the totals are made up of the same digit.

e Explain why the values can all be added together mentally.

f Each time the first number moves to the back of the queue, each of the other digits increases in value.

    i By how much does the 5 increase each time?

    ii By how much does the 8 increase each time?

    iii Explain why it is the same amount each time.

You will need:
• calculator

This 6-digit number is standing at the bus stop:

BUS STOP

791 864

If the first digit goes to the back of the queue, the new number will be:

BUS STOP

918 647

a Add together the two numbers above.

b Is the answer a multiple of 11? Use a calculator to find out.

c Choose a different 6-digit number. Move the first digit to the back of the queue and add the two numbers together. Is the answer a multiple of 11? Can you prove this always happens?

Adding mentally

- Add mentally, including with large numbers
- Use estimation to check answers

Challenge 1

Work out these calculations mentally. Show your working out.

a **376 154**

  i + 7000
  ii + 850
  iii + 42 000

b **603 147**

  i + 580
  ii + 31 000
  iii + 6000

c **568 743**

  i + 6000
  ii + 17 000
  iii + 630

d **750 862**

  i + 7100
  ii + 46 000
  iii + 460

e **862 774**

  i + 910
  ii + 5600
  iii + 51 000

f **937 927**

  i + 9000
  ii + 67 000
  iii + 580

Challenge 2

1 First estimate the answers to these calculations, then work them out mentally. Show your working out. Check your answer is close to your estimate.

a **2 387 590**

  i + 60 000
  ii + 300 000
  iii + 540

b **1 206 472**

  i + 43 000
  ii + 5100
  iii + 500 000

c **4 517 640**

  i + 950
  ii + 600 000
  iii + 4000

d **3 865 413**

  i + 400 000
  ii + 7200
  iii + 830

e **6 731 604**

  i + 840
  ii + 700 000
  iii + 3800

f **5 145 355**

  i + 5500
  ii + 400 000
  iii + 700

2 What has been added each time to reach the next number?

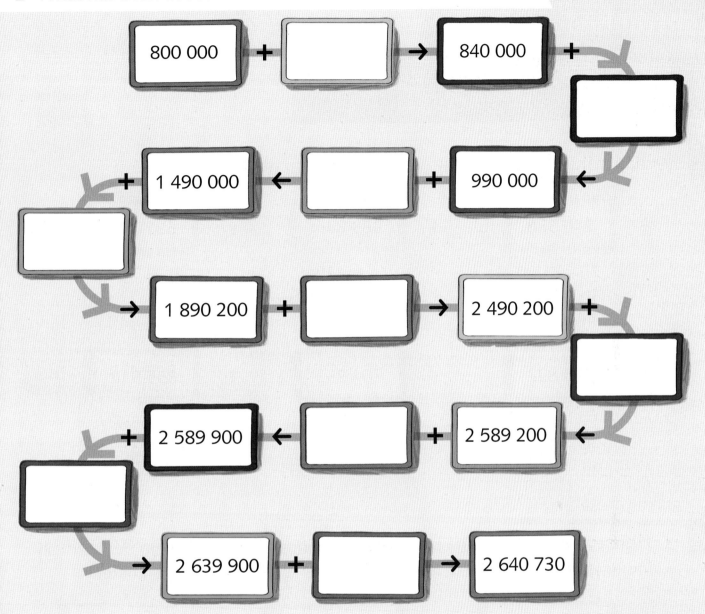

Work out the missing numbers mentally.

a 2 674 836 + _____ = 3 174 836   b 4 315 738 + _____ = 4 915 738

c 3 721 274 + _____ = 4 521 274   d 5 873 297 + _____ = 6 173 297

e 6 947 361 + _____ = 7 547 361   f 600 000 + _____ = 4 386 543

g 400 000 + _____ = 5 812 440   h 700 000 + _____ = 6 381 502

i 800 000 + _____ = 3 491 532   j 900 000 + _____ = 1 582 365

Subtracting mentally

- Subtract mentally, including with large numbers
- Use estimation to check answers

Challenge 1

Work out these calculations mentally. Show your working out.

a 248 386
  i – 4000
  ii – 230
  iii – 31 000

b 563 845
  i – 730
  ii – 45 000
  iii – 5000

c 681 378
  i – 7000
  ii – 27 000
  iii – 640

d 463 822
  i – 3100
  ii – 35 000
  iii – 750

e 754 233
  i – 580
  ii – 6200
  iii – 41 000

f 855 912
  i – 560
  ii – 38 000
  iii – 7100

Challenge 2

1 First estimate the answers to these calculations, then work them out mentally. Show your working out. Check your answer is close to your estimate.

a 3 763 282
  i – 50 000
  ii – 200 000
  iii – 240

b 4 738 295
  i – 29 000
  ii – 4800
  iii – 400 000

c 6 287 674
  i – 710
  ii – 400 000
  iii – 8000

d 7 590 217
  i – 600 000
  ii – 1200
  iii – 210

e 5 493 751
  i – 760
  ii – 700 000
  iii – 4800

f 8 691 302
  i – 25 000
  ii – 1200
  iii – 250

2 What has been subtracted each time to reach the next number?

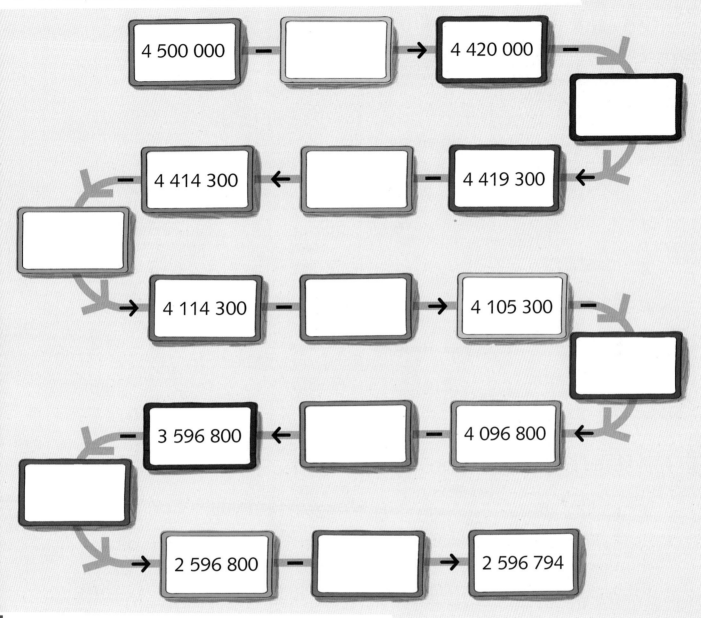

1 Work out the missing numbers mentally.

a $3\,428\,827 -$ ___ $= 2\,928\,827$ **b** $4\,398\,291 -$ ___ $= 3\,898\,291$

c $2\,864\,375 -$ ___ $= 2\,828\,375$ **d** $6\,721\,453 -$ ___ $= 6\,121\,453$

e $8\,836\,525 -$ ___ $= 7\,836\,525$ **f** $7\,329\,081 -$ ___ $= 6\,729\,081$

2 Explain how you worked out the missing numbers in Question 1.

3 When do you think mental calculations should be used and when should written calculations be used? In your opinion, is it important to learn how to do both? Explain why.

Adding and subtracting decimals

Add and subtract decimals mentally

Challenge 1

Add and subtract these decimals mentally.

a	37·4 + 25·8	**b**	19·7 + 42·6	**c**	39·8 + 45·4
d	68·9 + 32·7	**e**	61·4 + 56·8	**f**	72·3 + 45·9
g	38·6 + 73·5	**h**	59·4 + 57·9	**i**	65·3 + 78·4
j	62·4 − 38·2	**k**	71·6 − 53·4	**l**	85·6 − 31·8
m	74·1 − 46·5	**n**	87·5 − 27·8	**o**	90·2 − 53·4
p	72·7 − 48·8	**q**	95·3 − 68·6	**r**	52·4 − 28·6

Challenge 2

1 Add and subtract these decimals mentally.

a	63·48 + 29·29	**b**	39·63 + 52·48
c	58·26 + 57·5	**d**	97·8 + 32·19
e	61·48 + 79·59	**f**	87·4 + 95·98
g	89·08 + 76·97	**h**	65·4 + 92·63
i	58·32 − 31·53	**j**	62·47 − 45·82
k	71·61 − 55·4	**l**	86·4 − 27·51
m	94·13 − 45·35	**n**	82·38 − 37·5
o	72·2 − 33·86	**p**	99·04 − 48·37

Remember to use jottings to help you.

16

2 Each set of three circles total the number in the square. Find the missing numbers.

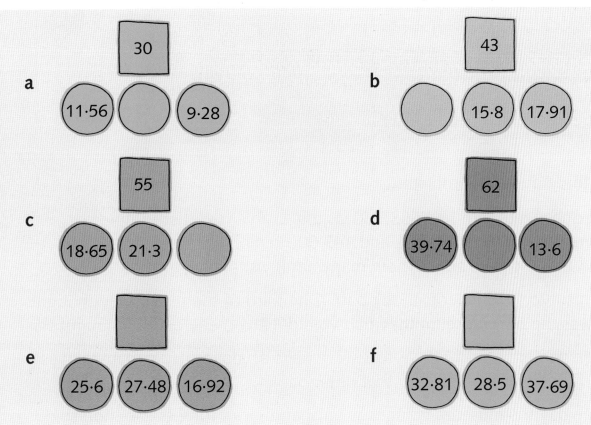

a
30
11·56 9·28

b
43
15·8 17·91

c
55
18·65 21·3

d
62
39·74 13·6

e
25·6 27·48 16·92

f
32·81 28·5 37·69

The decimal numbers on each side of the square total the number in the circle.
Find the missing numbers.

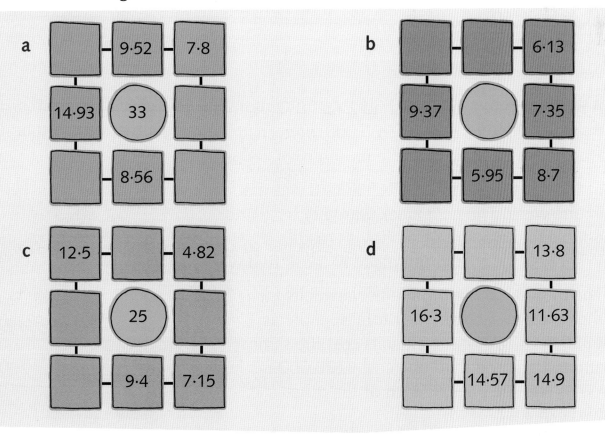

a
9·52 — 7·8
14·93 33
8·56

b
6·13
9·37 7·35
5·95 — 8·7

c
12·5 — 4·82
25
9·4 — 7·15

d
13·8
16·3 11·63
14·57 — 14·9

Museum problems

- Solve multi-step problems in contexts, deciding which operations and methods to use and why
- Use estimation to check accuracy of answers

Challenge 1

Answer these museum problems.

a A science museum had 653 760 visitors last year. If there were 230 000 child visitors and 147 000 senior citizens visitors and the rest were adults, how many adult visitors were there?

b In a survey, 4578 people took part. One third of them said they thought it was the best museum they had visited. How many people thought this?

c One winter's day, 5845 visitors wore pairs of gloves. How many gloves were there at the museum that day?

d One day the museum guide was on special offer for €3. The shop sold 936 copies. How much money was taken from the sale of these?

e On the busiest day of the year there were 7406 visitors. On the quietest day there were 1620 visitors. What was the difference between the visitor numbers on these two days?

Challenge 2

1 Answer these museum problems.

a A natural history museum had 2 653 812 visitors last year. A quarter of them were senior citizens, 900 000 were children and the rest were adults. How many adults visited the museum?

b In the gift shop, a profit of €5673.78 was made in one week. The next week was very busy and double that amount of profit was made. What was the total profit made in those two weeks?

c The museum bought three new exhibits for the dinosaur section. Their total spend was €856 400. Two of the exhibits cost the same amount and the third one cost €270 000. What was the price of each of the other two exhibits?

d The museum's budget for new signs is €6500. Each sign costs €6.
The museum buys as many signs as it can. How much money is left?

e The manager spent €768 429 on decorating the museum. He spent
€325 350 on the education centre and the rest on three of the exhibition
rooms. How much was spent on each exhibition room?

2 Write your own museum problems based on these calculations.

a 1 678 390 – 40 000 – 780

b 395 270 + 900 000 + 30 000

c €7629.25 + €2958.10 – €3861.02

Answer these museum problems.

a The museum manager is working out the visitor numbers for last year.
When he adds the children, senior citizens and adult visitor numbers together
it totals 3 652 780. When he adds the children and senior citizens together it
totals 1 976 000. When he adds the children and adults together it totals
2 376 788. How many of each kind of visitor were there?

b Heating and cooling the museum costs €23 475 for the three coldest months,
€18 781 for the three hottest months and €31 547 for the other six months.

   i What is the total annual bill?

   ii What is the average heating bill for one of the coldest months?

   iii The museum gets a 10% discount on its annual energy bill.
What is the new cost?

c The museum exceeds its gift shop sales target by 25%.
€450 000 was the total profit. What was the museum's target?

d After a trip to the museum, teachers at a school want to buy some books
to support their topics. They spend a total of €165.20.
€78.50 was spent on dinosaur books and
€35.99 on a very special Atlas. With the rest
of the money, they bought as many insect
books costing €12.30 as they could.
How much money was left?

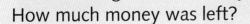

Building 3-D shapes

Build 3-D shapes from 2-D drawings

You will need:
- interlocking cubes in two colours

1 Look at the shapes below and write how many of each 2-D face the 3-D shapes have.

2-D faces

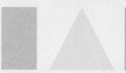

3-D shapes

a cuboid   **b** triangular prism   **c** cube

2 Build each shape below, in turn, with interlocking cubes of the same colour. Follow the instructions for each shape.
- Work out the least number of additional cubes you will need to make the shape into a cuboid.
- Using a different colour, add that number of cubes to the shape to check that you are correct. Write how many cubes you needed.

A 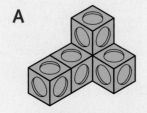   **B** 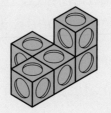   **C**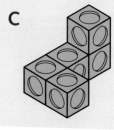

1 Build each shape below, in turn, with interlocking cubes of the same colour. Follow the instructions for each shape.
- Work out the least number of additional cubes you will need to make the shape into a cuboid.
- Using a different colour, add that number of cubes to the shape to check that you are correct. Write how many cubes you needed.

A 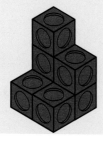   **B**    **C**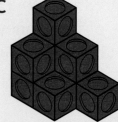

2 Build each shape below, in turn, with interlocking cubes of the same colour. Follow the instructions for each shape.

- For each shape, predict the least number of additional cubes you will need to build all the layers of the shape up to one level higher than the highest end.
- Using a different colour, add that number of cubes to the shape to check that you are correct. Write how many cubes you needed.

A
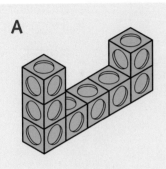

B
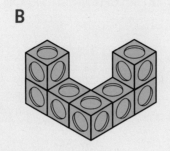

C
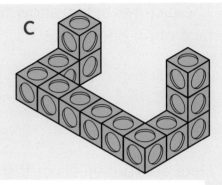

1 Work with a partner. Build each tower, in turn, with interlocking cubes of the same colour. Follow the instructions for each shape.

- Work out the least number of additional cubes you will need to make each tower into a cube.
- Using a different colour, add that number of cubes to the tower to check that you are correct.

A
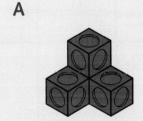

B
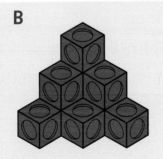

C
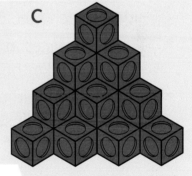

2 Use your work from Question 1 to answer the questions.

a Copy and complete the table.

Shape	Number of cubes in tower	Number of cubes added	Total number of cubes
A			8 or 2 x 2 x 2
B			
C			

b Look for a pattern. Work out the total number of cubes needed to build cube D.

Nets of open and closed cubes

Identify and build different nets for an open or a closed cube

 Challenge 1

The pictures below show five different designs on each face of an open cube.

Here are four views of the open cube:

- Copy the net on the right onto 1 cm squared paper. Make the side of each face 5 cm long.
- Draw the faces in the correct place to make the open cube.
- Cut out and fold up the net to check your answer.

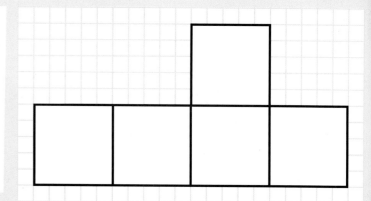

You will need:
- 1 cm squared paper
- ruler
- scissors

 Challenge 2

Some of the shapes on the opposite page are nets of closed cubes.

- Copy the table below.
- Make each shape, in turn, with your interlocking squares. Then fold the shape up to see if it makes a cube.
- For each shape, enter ✓ if the shape is a net of a cube and ✗ if it is not.

You will need:
- six interlocking squares

Shape	A	B	C	D	E	F	G	H	I	J	K	L
Net of a cube												

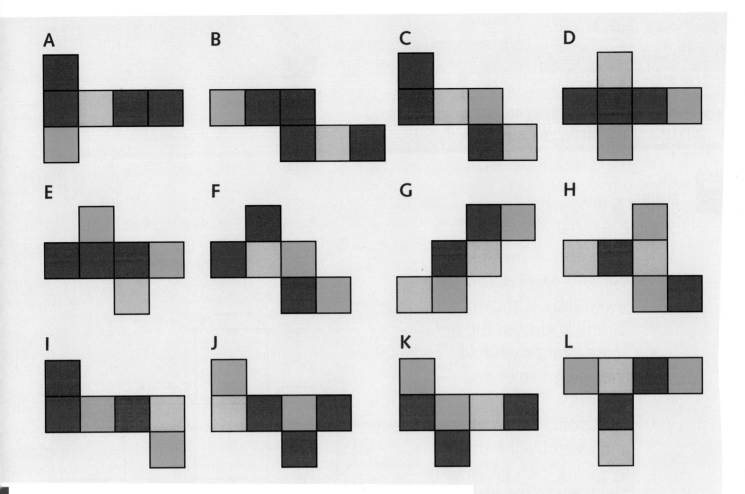

Make two copies of each of the nets below onto 1 cm square paper. Make the side of each face 5 cm long. Each one is the net of an open cube. The coloured square indicates the bottom face.

- For each net find two different ways to add one square and turn it into the net of a closed cube.

- Cut out each net, with the square added, and check that it will fold into a cube.

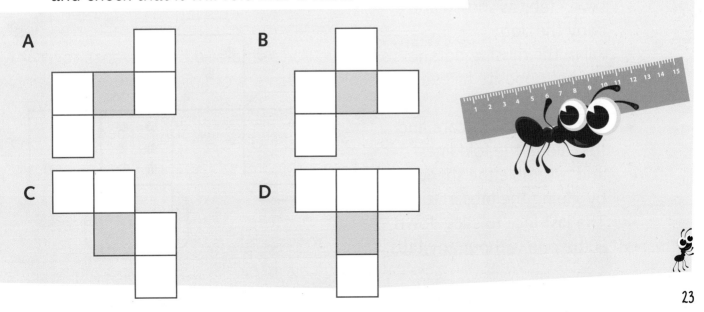

Nets of a cube and a cuboid

Construct nets for a cube and a cuboid

You will need:
- 1 cm square dot grid paper
- ruler
- scissors
- glue

Challenge 1

Build a cube.

- Copy the net of the cube onto 1 cm square dot grid paper. Draw the seven tabs as shown.
- Carefully cut out the net.
- Score along each fold line using a ruler and scissors.
- Fold along each fold line and assemble the shape by gluing each tab in turn. The last face to stick down is the one without any tabs.

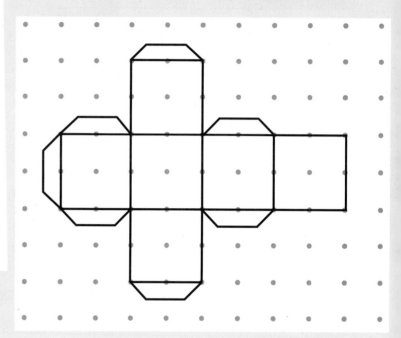

Challenge 2

1 Build a dice.

- Copy the net of the dice onto 1 cm square dot grid paper. Draw the seven tabs as shown and copy the dots.
- Fill in the missing dots so that opposite faces add to 7.
- Cut out the net, score and fold along the fold lines and assemble the shape by gluing the tabs in turn. The last face to stick down is the one without any tabs.

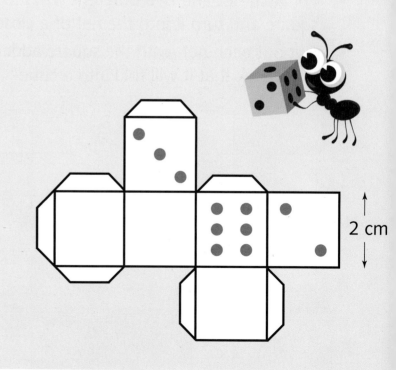

2 cm

2 Build a cuboid.

- Using the lengths of sides as shown in the diagram, copy the net of the cuboid onto 1 cm square dot grid paper.
- Decide where to draw the seven tabs.
- Cut out the net, score and fold along the fold lines and assemble the shape by gluing the tabs in turn. The last face to stick down is the one without any tabs.

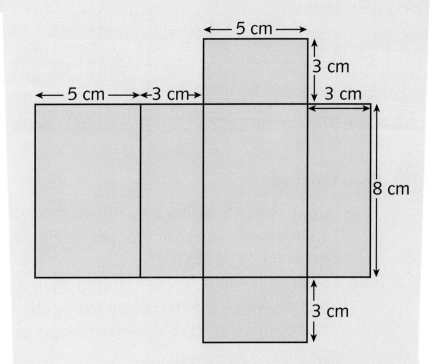

The edges of this cube measure 2 cm.
A spot covers one vertex of the cube.

For each of the nets below:

- copy the net onto 1 cm square dot grid paper
- add the two remaining parts of the spot so that the three parts will meet at the same vertex when the cube is made up
- decide where to draw the seven tabs
- cut out the nets and fold them up to check your spots match up

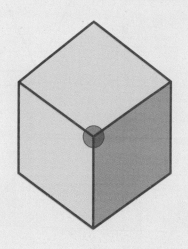

A   B   C

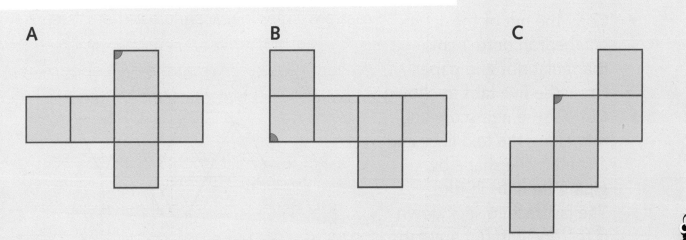

Nets for 3-D shapes with triangular faces

Draw nets for shapes with one or more triangular faces

Build tetrahedons.

- Copy the nets below of a tetrahedron onto 1 cm triangular dot grid paper. Draw each set of three tabs as shown.
- Cut out the nets, score and fold along the fold lines and assemble the shapes by gluing the tabs in turn. The last face to stick down is the one without any tabs.

You will need:
- 1 cm triangular dot grid paper
- ruler
- scissors
- glue

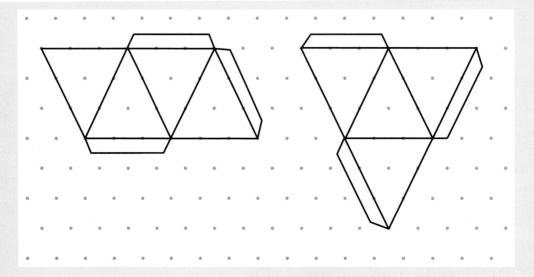

1 Build an octahedron.

- Copy the net of the octahedron onto 1 cm triangular dot grid paper. Draw the five tabs as shown.
- Cut out the net, score and fold along the fold lines and assemble the shape by gluing the tabs in turn. The last face to stick down is the one without any tabs.

You will need:
- 1 cm triangular dot grid paper • ruler
- scissors • glue • coloured pencils

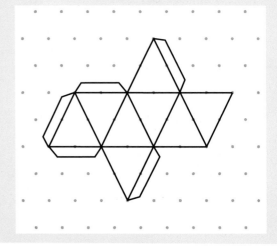

2 Work with a partner. Each person should copy and cut out the net below. Find a way to stick both of your shapes together to make a 'snap dragon' octahedron. Add the teeth and the eyes.

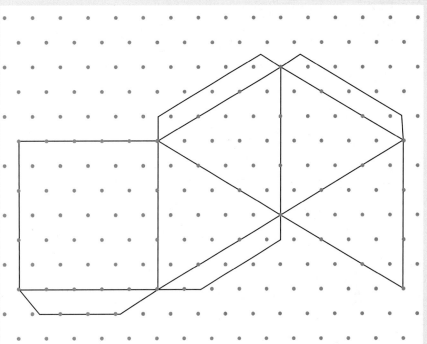

1 Work with a partner. Each person should construct a square-based pyramid using the net shown.

- Draw a square with sides of 6 cm.
- Using your ruler and protractor, draw an equilateral triangle with sides of 6 cm on each side of the square.
- Draw a tab on one side of each triangle.
- Cut out the net, score and fold along the fold lines and glue the tabs in turn to form the square-based pyramid.

You will need:
- sheet of paper
- protractor
- ruler
- scissors
- glue

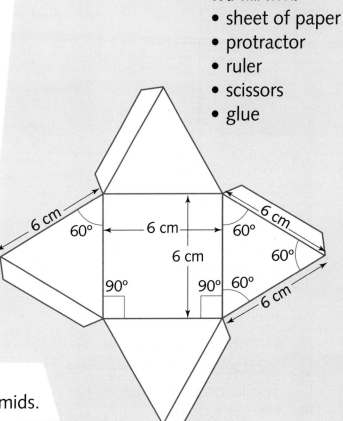

2 Name the 3-D shape you can make using both of your square-based pyramids.

Multiplying ThHTO × 0

- Use the formal written method of short multiplication to calculate ThHTO × O
- Estimate and check the answer to a calculation

Example

50 × 9 = 450

Challenge 1

Write the multiplication fact for each number in the sets below.

× 9

90   50
300   80
700   6
40   1200
20   110

× 7

50   600
300   8
400   7
900   80
1100   12

× 6

700   90
80   12
6   50
400   600
120   110

Challenge 2

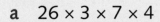

1 Find the answer to these calculations.

a 26 × 3 × 7 × 4   b 64 × 6 × 8   c 53 × 5 × 4

d 32 × 6 × 8 × 4   e 27 × 5 × 9 × 6   f 47 × 9 × 8 × 3

g 68 × 4 × 9 × 9   h 25 × 5 × 5 × 5   i 17 × 6 × 4 × 9

2 Play this game with a partner.

Take turns to:

You will need:
- 0–9 dice

- Choose a number from the number cards below and write it down (you can only use each number once).
- Roll the dice.
- Multiply your chosen number by the number rolled on the dice, estimating your answer first.
- Calculate the answer using the formal written method.
- Check that your answer is close to your estimate.

The player with the highest answer scores one point.
The first player to score five points is the winner.

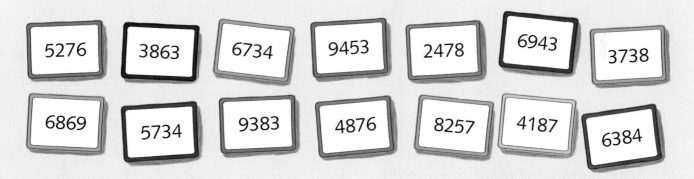

5276 3863 6734 9453 2478 6943 3738

6869 5734 9383 4876 8257 4187 6384

Work out the missing numbers in these calculations.

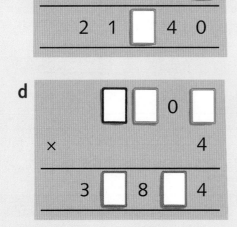

a
```
    □ 3 □ 8
  ×       □
  ─────────
  2 1 □ 4 0
```

b
```
    6 □ 6 □
  ×       7
  ─────────
  4 □ 3 □ 9
```

c
```
    □ 5 0 □
  ×       □
  ─────────
  6 7 5 5 4
```

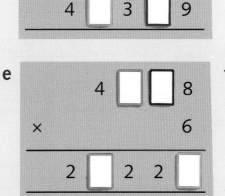

d
```
    □ □ 0 □
  ×       4
  ─────────
  3 □ 8 □ 4
```

e
```
    4 □ □ 8
  ×       6
  ─────────
  2 □ 2 2 □
```

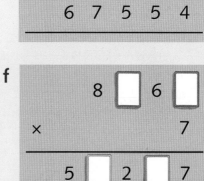

f
```
    8 □ 6 □
  ×       7
  ─────────
  5 □ 2 □ 7
```

Multiplication TO × TO using the expanded written method

- Use the expanded written method to calculate TO × TO
- Estimate and check the answer to a calculation

Challenge 1

Work out these multiplication calculations.

1. a 8 × 3
   b 80 × 30
   c 8 × 30

2. a 9 × 8
   b 80 × 9
   c 90 × 80

3. a 7 × 4
   b 70 × 4
   c 40 × 70

4. a 8 × 6
   b 6 × 80
   c 80 × 60

5. a 8 × 8
   b 80 × 80
   c 80 × 8

6. a 9 × 30
   b 3 × 9
   c 30 × 90

7. a 6 × 5
   b 60 × 5
   c 60 × 50

8. a 7 × 8
   b 70 × 80
   c 80 × 70

Challenge 2

1. Choose a number from each box below and create a multiplication calculation. Estimate the answer first. Multiply the numbers together using the expanded written method. Then compare your answer with your estimate. Choose different numbers each time. Write at least eight calculations. Choose the method that is easiest for you.

Example

Th	H	T	O	
		4	3	
×		3	8	
	3	4²	4	(43 × 8)
1	2	9	0	(43 × 30)
1	6	3	4	
			1	

Th	H	T	O	
		4	3	
×		3	8	
1	2	9	0	(43 × 30
	3	4²	4	(43 × 8)
1	6	3	4	
			1	

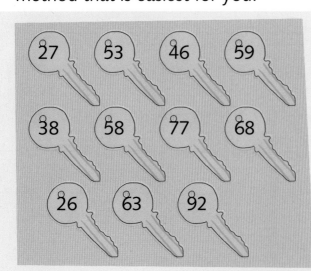

Keys: 27, 53, 46, 59, 38, 58, 77, 68, 26, 63, 92

Locks: 36, 48, 39, 43, 62, 84, 57, 93, 69, 43, 67

2 Make your own TO × TO calculations. Choose any two numbers from below. Multiply them together. Choose another two numbers. Multiply them together. Multiply the answers from both of your calculations to get your final answer. Try this five times.

Use each of the number cards once. Make a calculation that gives the answer shown.

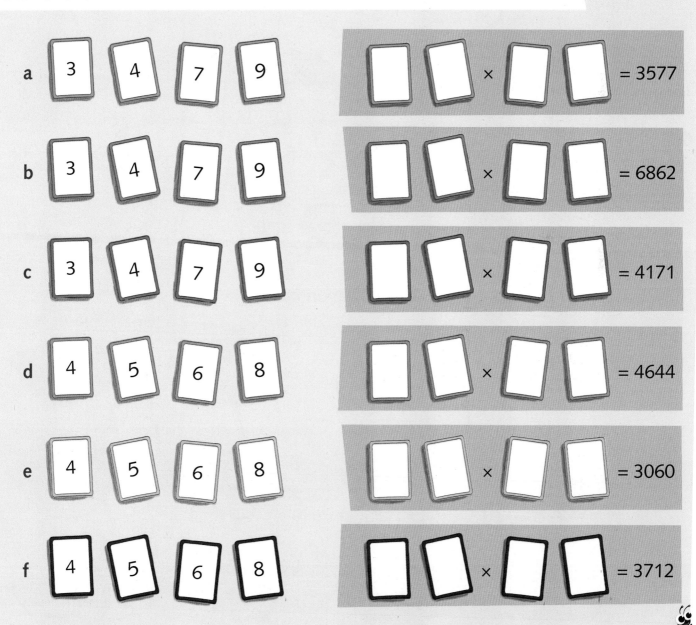

Multiplication TO × TO using the formal written method

- Use the formal written method of long multiplication to calculate TO × TO
- Estimate and check the answer to a calculation

1 Work out the missing number in each multiplication fact.

a   7 × 9 =

b   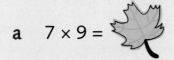 × 7 = 49

c   8 × 6 =

d   9 ×   = 108

e   4 ×   = 48

f   7 ×   = 42

g   6 ×   = 54

h   × 8 = 72

i   × 8 = 32

j   9 ×   = 63

k   7 ×   = 28

l   6 ×   = 36

2 Work out the answer to each calculation mentally.

a   60 × 7

b   50 × 80

c   60 × 8

d   9 × 70

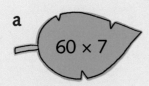
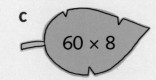

e   80 × 9

f   80 × 7

g   3 × 80

h   90 × 50

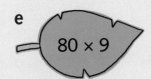
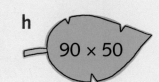

i   60 × 90

j   40 × 40

k   70 × 60

l   30 × 40

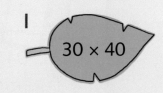

Estimate the answer first, then use the formal written method to find the answer to each calculation.

Example

Th	H	T	O
		4	6
×		3	8
	3	6⁴	8
1	3¹	8	0
1	7	4	8
	1		

a 45 × 42

b 68 × 68

c 76 × 67

d 38 × 49

e 57 × 39

f 61 × 83

g 72 × 51

h 87 × 58

i 76 × 77

j 26 × 64

k 37 × 78

l 84 × 48

m 55 × 55

n 65 × 56

o 18 × 81

1 Find the missing digits in each calculation.

a ☐7 × 3☐ = 891

b 2☐ × 84 = ☐184

c 36 × 6☐ = 2☐48

d 38 × ☐9 = 1862

e ☐6 × 56 = 3136

f 4☐ × 47 = 2021

g 29 × ☐1 = 2059

h 35 × ☐☐ = 8☐5

2 Find two different TO × TO calculations that give each of these answers.

| 1944 | 896 | 1012 | 720 | 988 |

Solving word problems (1)

Solve problems involving addition, subtraction, multiplication and division

Challenge 1

Copy each calculation and write in the missing sign.

a 60 ☐ 80 = 4800   b 600 = 12 ☐ 50

c 10 = 90 ☐ 80   d 1500 ☐ 300 = 1200

e 640 ☐ 80 = 8   f 70 ☐ 80 = 5600

g 3 ☐ 80 = 240   h 760 ☐ 120 = 880

i 310 ☐ 30 = 280   j 120 ☐ 30 = 4

k 480 ☐ 8 = 60   l 500 ☐ 50 = 10

$+$ $-$ $\div$ $\times$

Challenge 2

A school has to purchase some new items. Find the answer to each question.

€49
kettle

€38
globe

€36
set of 6 novels

€28
box of paints

€56
telephone

€39
tennis racquet

a The school buys 48 novels altogether. How much does it spend?

b A school buys 24 globes. How much change does the school receive from €1000?

c The supplier has a sale: 'Buy one get one half price'. The school office buys 6 kettles. How much is spent?

d It is decided that each classroom should have a telephone. There are 24 classrooms. What is the total cost?

e Tennis racquets are on sale at one third off their original price. If the school buys 36, how much does it spend?

f One of each item is purchased. What is the total cost?

g Novels are sold separately for €7 each. The library buys 3465 separate novels over the year. What is the total cost?

h Your class has a budget of €500 to spend. What would you buy?

1 Using the information in Challenge 2, find the answers to these problems.

a Janet buys two of the same item. She pays with two €50 notes and gets €24 change. What item does she buy?

b The two Year 6 classes spend the same amount of money on items. One class buys 3 boxes of paints. The other class buys 2 different items totalling the same amount of money. What items did they buy?

c All of the items shown are on sale at a 10% discount. What is the new price of each item? Record each calculation you use.

2 Investigate the following TO × TO puzzle.

- Look carefully at the digits in these two calculations. What do you notice?

$$48 \times 42 \qquad 24 \times 84$$

- Find the answer to both of the calculations. What do you notice?
- Find the missing digits in this pair of calculations so the same thing happens.

$$3\boxed{\ } \times 4\boxed{\ } \qquad \boxed{\ }4 \times \boxed{\ }3$$

- Can you make your own pairs of calculations that follow the same rule and have the same answer?

Fractions, factors and multiples (1)

Use common factors to simplify fractions; use common multiples to express fractions in the same denomination

Challenge 1

1 Simplify these fractions.

Example

$$\frac{12}{15} = \frac{4}{5}$$

Both numbers have a factor of 3, so if I divide them both by 3, I get the simplified fraction $\frac{4}{5}$.

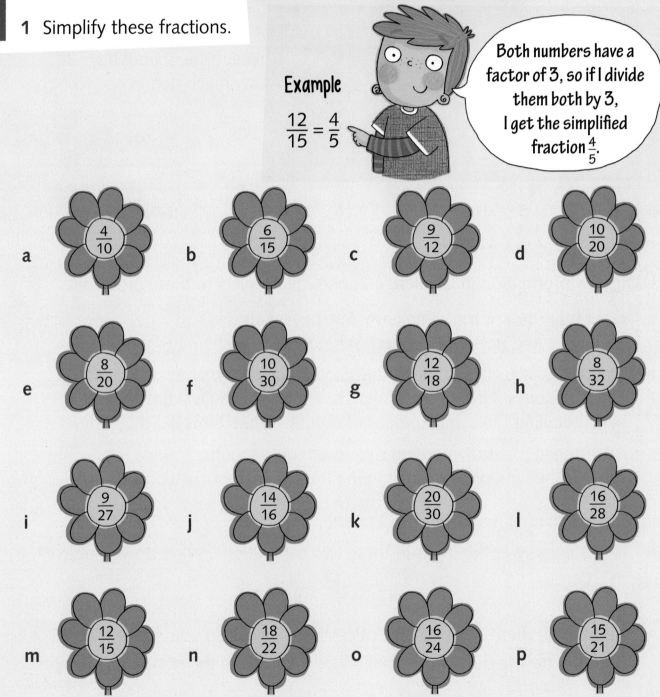

a $\frac{4}{10}$ b $\frac{6}{15}$ c $\frac{9}{12}$ d $\frac{10}{20}$

e $\frac{8}{20}$ f $\frac{10}{30}$ g $\frac{12}{18}$ h $\frac{8}{32}$

i $\frac{9}{27}$ j $\frac{14}{16}$ k $\frac{20}{30}$ l $\frac{16}{28}$

m $\frac{12}{15}$ n $\frac{18}{22}$ o $\frac{16}{24}$ p $\frac{15}{21}$

2 Write some fractions for a partner to simplify. Make sure you know the answers!

1 Play this game with a partner.

- Choose one of the fractions below and both write it down.
- Take turns to roll the dice.
- Simplify the fraction by the number you roll. If you cannot, wait for your next turn.
- Keep going until one player has the simplest form of the fraction. This scores one point.
- Play again, choosing other fractions from below. The first player to reach five points is the winner.

You will need:
- 1–6 dice

$$\frac{40}{60} \qquad \frac{48}{60} \qquad \frac{24}{30} \qquad \frac{30}{42} \qquad \frac{24}{40}$$

$$\frac{36}{48} \qquad \frac{56}{80} \qquad \frac{18}{36} \qquad \frac{50}{60} \qquad \frac{48}{80}$$

2 Choose two of the fractions below and change them to fractions with the same denominators. Do this ten times with different pairs of fractions. Fractions can be used more than once, but not in the same pair.

Example

$\frac{7}{10}$ and $\frac{4}{15}$

$= \frac{21}{30}$ and $\frac{8}{30}$

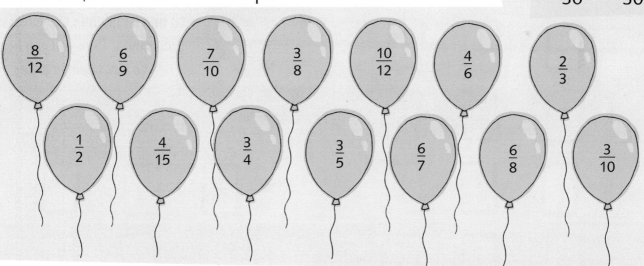

$$\frac{8}{12} \qquad \frac{6}{9} \qquad \frac{7}{10} \qquad \frac{3}{8} \qquad \frac{10}{12} \qquad \frac{4}{6} \qquad \frac{2}{3}$$

$$\frac{1}{2} \qquad \frac{4}{15} \qquad \frac{3}{4} \qquad \frac{3}{5} \qquad \frac{6}{7} \qquad \frac{6}{8} \qquad \frac{3}{10}$$

1 What is a simplified fraction?

2 Explain why $\frac{13}{15}$ cannot be simplified.

3 Roll the dice four times and record your digits. If you roll zero, roll the dice again. Use the digits to make two proper fractions. Look at the denominators. Express the fractions as two fractions with the same denominator.

You will need:
- 0–9 dice

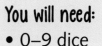

Ordering fractions

Compare and order fractions, including fractions greater than 1

Challenge 1

1 Order the fractions in each set, smallest to largest.

Example

$\frac{3}{4}$ → 4, 8, __12__ $\frac{3}{4} = \frac{9}{12}$

$\frac{2}{3}$ → 3, 6, 9, __12__ $\frac{2}{3} = \frac{8}{12}$

$\frac{1}{2}$ → 2, 4, 6, 8, 10, __12__ $\frac{1}{2} = \frac{6}{12}$

$\frac{1}{2}, \frac{2}{3}, \frac{3}{4}$

a $\frac{5}{6}$ $\frac{2}{3}$ $\frac{9}{12}$

b $\frac{1}{2}$ $\frac{5}{8}$ $\frac{3}{4}$

c $\frac{4}{6}$ $\frac{5}{9}$ $\frac{1}{3}$

d $\frac{1}{4}$ $\frac{3}{8}$ $\frac{2}{12}$

e $\frac{3}{5}$ $\frac{4}{10}$ $\frac{1}{2}$

f $\frac{3}{4}$ $\frac{7}{12}$ $\frac{2}{3}$

Remember to count on in steps of the denominator, to find a multiple they all have in common. Then you can begin to put them in order.

g $\frac{4}{7}$ $\frac{2}{3}$ $\frac{1}{2}$ **h** $\frac{4}{10}$ $\frac{1}{4}$ $\frac{2}{5}$

i $\frac{13}{16}$ $\frac{7}{8}$ $\frac{3}{4}$ **j** $\frac{2}{6}$ $\frac{3}{8}$ $\frac{1}{4}$

k $\frac{7}{10}$ $\frac{3}{5}$ $\frac{3}{4}$ **l** $\frac{4}{9}$ $\frac{1}{3}$ $\frac{1}{4}$

2 Write a set of instructions explaining how to order fractions so you can remember how to do it.

1 For each set of fractions below, predict their order, smallest to largest, without converting them.

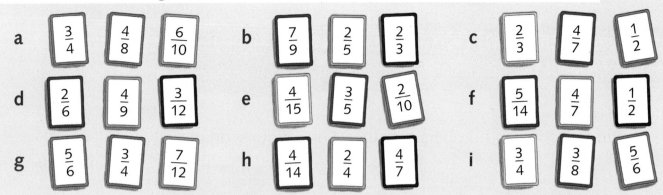

a $\frac{3}{4}$ $\frac{4}{8}$ $\frac{6}{10}$ b $\frac{7}{9}$ $\frac{2}{5}$ $\frac{2}{3}$ c $\frac{2}{3}$ $\frac{4}{7}$ $\frac{1}{2}$

d $\frac{2}{6}$ $\frac{4}{9}$ $\frac{3}{12}$ e $\frac{4}{15}$ $\frac{3}{5}$ $\frac{2}{10}$ f $\frac{5}{14}$ $\frac{4}{7}$ $\frac{1}{2}$

g $\frac{5}{6}$ $\frac{3}{4}$ $\frac{7}{12}$ h $\frac{4}{14}$ $\frac{2}{4}$ $\frac{4}{7}$ i $\frac{3}{4}$ $\frac{3}{8}$ $\frac{5}{6}$

2 Order each set of fractions in Question 1 by finding their lowest common denominator. Check to see if your predictions were close.

3 Order these improper fractions.

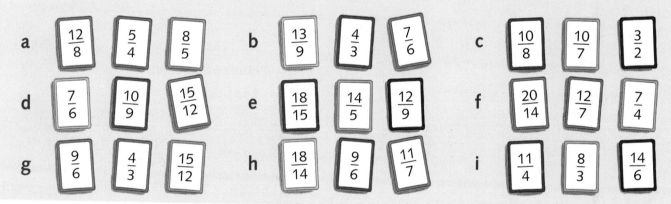

a $\frac{12}{8}$ $\frac{5}{4}$ $\frac{8}{5}$ b $\frac{13}{9}$ $\frac{4}{3}$ $\frac{7}{6}$ c $\frac{10}{8}$ $\frac{10}{7}$ $\frac{3}{2}$

d $\frac{7}{6}$ $\frac{10}{9}$ $\frac{15}{12}$ e $\frac{18}{15}$ $\frac{14}{5}$ $\frac{12}{9}$ f $\frac{20}{14}$ $\frac{12}{7}$ $\frac{7}{4}$

g $\frac{9}{6}$ $\frac{4}{3}$ $\frac{15}{12}$ h $\frac{18}{14}$ $\frac{9}{6}$ $\frac{11}{7}$ i $\frac{11}{4}$ $\frac{8}{3}$ $\frac{14}{6}$

Some proper fractions have been muddled up. Some of the numbers below are numerators and some are denominators of proper fractions that have been separated.

24　4　9　11　6　2　12　5　88　27　3　15

a Make a set of proper fractions using all the cards. Order your fractions, smallest to largest, by finding their common denominator.

b What were the smallest and largest fractions you could make?

c Look at your fractions again. Can you order them without converting them to common denominators?

d What strategy did you use to order your fractions in Question **c**? Compare your fractions and your strategy with a partner's. Did you make the same fractions?

Adding fractions

Add fractions with different denominators and mixed numbers, using the concept of equivalent fractions

Challenge 1

1 Add these mixed numbers together. Show your working.

a $3\frac{2}{5} + 7\frac{1}{5}$

b $5\frac{1}{4} + 7\frac{2}{4}$

c $6\frac{5}{8} + 4\frac{2}{8}$

d $7\frac{3}{9} + 6\frac{5}{9}$

e $5\frac{4}{10} + 3\frac{5}{10}$

f $2\frac{2}{3} + 5\frac{1}{3}$

g $8\frac{2}{7} + 6\frac{4}{7}$

h $9\frac{1}{2} + 5\frac{1}{2}$

i $5\frac{3}{12} + 4\frac{5}{12}$

j $7\frac{5}{11} + 8\frac{5}{11}$

Example

$2\frac{3}{6} + 5\frac{2}{6}$

$2 + 5 = 7$

$\frac{3}{6} + \frac{2}{6} = \frac{5}{6}$

$7 + \frac{5}{6} = 7\frac{5}{6}$

Add the whole numbers and then the fractions.

2 Add these fractions and then convert the answer to a mixed number.

a $\frac{3}{4} + \frac{3}{4}$

b $\frac{4}{5} + \frac{3}{5}$

c $\frac{5}{7} + \frac{4}{7}$

d $\frac{7}{8} + \frac{3}{8}$

e $\frac{7}{9} + \frac{7}{9}$

f $\frac{4}{7} + \frac{6}{7}$

g $\frac{8}{10} + \frac{6}{10}$

h $\frac{9}{11} + \frac{5}{11}$

i $\frac{7}{12} + \frac{6}{12}$

Example

$\frac{3}{6} + \frac{5}{6} = \frac{8}{6}$

$\frac{8}{6} = 1\frac{2}{6} = 1\frac{1}{3}$

Challenge 2

1 Add these mixed numbers together.

a $3\frac{4}{5} + 6\frac{3}{5}$

b $2\frac{6}{8} + 4\frac{5}{8}$

c $6\frac{2}{3} + 8\frac{2}{3}$

d $5\frac{4}{9} + 7\frac{6}{9}$

e $6\frac{7}{10} + 8\frac{5}{10}$

f $9\frac{3}{4} + 5\frac{3}{4}$

g $3\frac{11}{13} + 6\frac{2}{13}$

h $8\frac{4}{7} + 5\frac{6}{7}$

i $9\frac{8}{12} + 7\frac{5}{12}$

j $3\frac{6}{13} + 7\frac{11}{13}$

2 Choose two of the mixed numbers below and add them together. Do this ten times. The mixed numbers can be used more than once, but not in the same pair.

Hint

First convert the fractions to equivalent fractions with the same denominator.

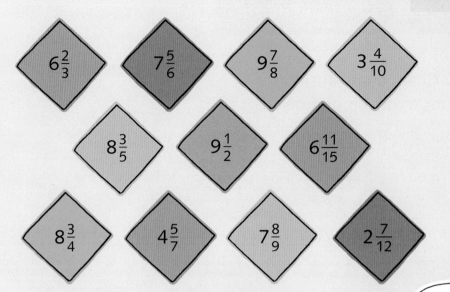

Example

$7\frac{2}{3} + 3\frac{7}{8}$

$7 + 3 = 10$

$\frac{2}{3} + \frac{7}{8} = \frac{16}{24} + \frac{21}{24}$

$= \frac{37}{24}$

$= 1\frac{13}{24}$

$10 + 1\frac{13}{24} = 11\frac{13}{24}$

3 Which combinations of mixed numbers in Question 2 did you find easiest to add? Explain why.

Check that your answers are simplified to the lowest form.

1 Add these improper fractions. Write each answer as a mixed number.

a $\frac{5}{3} + \frac{4}{3}$ b $\frac{6}{8} + \frac{7}{8}$ c $\frac{9}{4} + \frac{5}{4}$ d $\frac{7}{5} + \frac{8}{5}$ e $\frac{3}{2} + \frac{5}{2}$

f $\frac{9}{6} + \frac{7}{6}$ g $\frac{12}{10} + \frac{15}{10}$ h $\frac{11}{5} + \frac{9}{5}$ i $\frac{8}{4} + \frac{9}{4}$ j $\frac{15}{12} + \frac{14}{12}$

2 Choose three of the mixed numbers below and add them together. Do this five times. The mixed numbers can be used more than once.

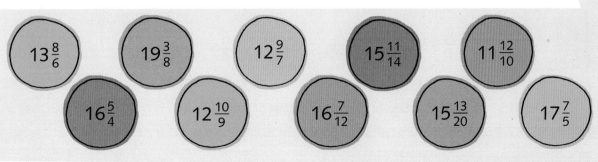

3 Which combinations of mixed numbers in Question 2 did you find easiest to add? Explain why.

Subtracting fractions

Subtract fractions with different denominators and mixed numbers, using the concept of equivalent fractions

Challenge 1

1 Subtract these fractions. Change any answers that are improper fractions to mixed numbers.

Example
$$\frac{7}{4} - \frac{2}{4} = \frac{5}{4} = 1\frac{1}{4}$$

a $\frac{9}{5} - \frac{3}{5}$ b $\frac{10}{8} - \frac{4}{8}$ c $\frac{8}{6} - \frac{4}{6}$ d $\frac{12}{7} - \frac{3}{7}$ e $\frac{6}{4} - \frac{1}{4}$

f $\frac{5}{3} - \frac{2}{3}$ g $\frac{11}{9} - \frac{6}{9}$ h $\frac{3}{2} - \frac{2}{2}$ i $\frac{13}{8} - \frac{7}{8}$ j $\frac{14}{11} - \frac{8}{11}$

2 Subtract these mixed numbers. Show your working.

Example
$$5\frac{4}{6} - 2\frac{2}{6}$$
$$5 - 2 = 3$$
$$\frac{4}{6} - \frac{2}{6} = \frac{2}{6}$$
$$3 + \frac{2}{6} = 3\frac{2}{6} = 3\frac{1}{3}$$

a $7\frac{5}{8} - 2\frac{3}{8}$ b $5\frac{4}{7} - 2\frac{1}{7}$ c $8\frac{3}{4} - 3\frac{1}{4}$

d $7\frac{9}{10} - 6\frac{4}{10}$ e $9\frac{4}{5} - 2\frac{3}{5}$ f $7\frac{5}{6} - 3\frac{4}{6}$

g $8\frac{7}{9} - 4\frac{2}{9}$ h $4\frac{1}{2} - 2\frac{1}{2}$

Subtract the whole numbers and then the fractions.

i $7\frac{3}{12} - 5\frac{1}{12}$ j $9\frac{6}{10} - 9\frac{2}{10}$

Challenge 2

1 Subtract these mixed numbers. The first mixed number will need changing, as shown in the example.

Example
$$4\frac{3}{5} - 2\frac{4}{5} = 3\frac{3+5}{5} - 2\frac{4}{5} = 3\frac{8}{5} - 2\frac{4}{5} = 1\frac{4}{5}$$

a $5\frac{3}{7} - 2\frac{5}{7}$ b $8\frac{2}{5} - 3\frac{4}{5}$

c $7\frac{3}{8} - 4\frac{7}{8}$ d $9\frac{1}{6} - 5\frac{4}{6}$ e $7\frac{1}{3} - 4\frac{2}{3}$ f $10\frac{5}{9} - 4\frac{7}{9}$

g $12\frac{1}{4} - 8\frac{3}{4}$ h $15\frac{2}{6} - 11\frac{4}{6}$ i $10\frac{2}{12} - 5\frac{7}{12}$ j $11\frac{1}{8} - 3\frac{2}{8}$

2 Subtract these mixed numbers. First convert the fractions to equivalent fractions with the same denominator.

a $\left(6\frac{3}{4} - 2\frac{2}{6}\right)$ b $\left(7\frac{2}{3} - 4\frac{1}{4}\right)$ c $\left(9\frac{4}{5} - 3\frac{4}{15}\right)$

Example

$7\frac{6}{8} - 5\frac{5}{12}$

$7 - 5 = 2$

$\frac{6}{8} - \frac{5}{12} = \frac{18}{24} - \frac{10}{24}$

$\qquad = \frac{8}{24} = \frac{1}{3}$

$\frac{1}{3} + 2 = 2\frac{1}{3}$

d $\left(8\frac{6}{8} - 1\frac{3}{12}\right)$ e $\left(9\frac{8}{10} - 2\frac{3}{4}\right)$ f $\left(10\frac{6}{7} - 3\frac{1}{2}\right)$

g $\left(12\frac{7}{9} - 5\frac{2}{6}\right)$ h $\left(11\frac{3}{4} - 4\frac{2}{5}\right)$

Check your answers are in the simplest form.

i $\left(16\frac{6}{7} - 11\frac{1}{3}\right)$ j $\left(14\frac{8}{9} - 5\frac{3}{4}\right)$

1 Look at the calculations in Question 2, below. Predict the calculations where the first mixed number will need changing, even after you have found the common denominator. Write the letters of these calculations in your book. Choose one of them and explain how you knew.

2 Work out these calculations.

a $\boxed{11\frac{3}{5} - 3\frac{2}{10}}$ b $\boxed{9\frac{3}{4} - 5\frac{2}{5}}$ c $\boxed{13\frac{1}{6} - 7\frac{5}{9}}$ d $\boxed{15\frac{7}{10} - 8\frac{3}{15}}$

e $\boxed{12\frac{7}{12} - 4\frac{1}{2}}$ f $\boxed{16\frac{4}{7} - 10\frac{2}{3}}$ g $\boxed{21\frac{4}{5} - 17\frac{2}{6}}$ h $\boxed{19\frac{2}{6} - 12\frac{1}{7}}$

i $\boxed{20\frac{1}{2} - 14\frac{2}{5}}$ j $\boxed{21\frac{4}{5} - 8\frac{3}{9}}$ k $\boxed{16\frac{5}{8} - 13\frac{2}{3}}$ l $\boxed{22\frac{3}{5} - 18\frac{7}{15}}$

3 Write a set of instructions for subtracting mixed numbers. Include instructions for when the fractions have different denominators and when the first fraction needs changing.

Using coordinates to locate shapes (1)

Use coordinates to describe positions in two and in four quadrants and predict missing coordinates

Challenge 1

1 The points on the grid represent five footballers on a football pitch. Write the coordinates of players A to E.

2 The ball is at the point X (–2, 3).

Decide where to position the referee and write the coordinates as R (,). Explain your choice.

Challenge 2

1 The Cup Final has gone to a penalty shoot-out.

- The shot is a miss if the goalkeeper covers the coordinates.

- The shot is a goal if the coordinates are not covered by the goalkeeper.

a Copy and complete the score sheet for each team.

Rustean Rovers					
Coordinates of shot	(–2, 4)	(–5, 6)	(3, 4)	(–4, 1)	(2, 2)
Result	miss				

Ashwell United					
Coordinates of shot	(3, 5)	(–6, 1)	(–1, 2)	(3, 4)	(–3, 3)
Result					

b Which team won the Cup?

2 List the coordinates of the vertices of each shape.

  a square ABCD   **b** rectangle EFGH   **c** parallelogram KLMN

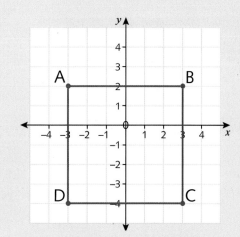
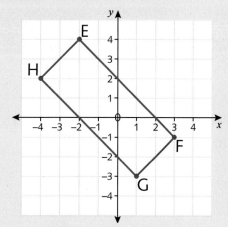
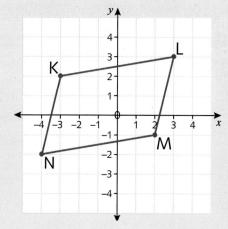

3 The points R, S and T form three of the vertices of a rhombus.

What are the coordinates of the fourth vertex U?

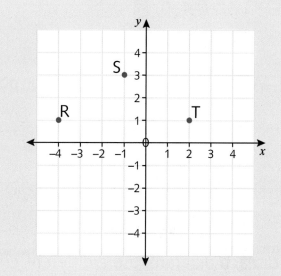

1 List the coordinates of the four points that are the vertices of:

  a a square

  b two parallelograms

  c an isosceles triangle with all angles less than 90°.

2 The points D (3, 2) and F (−1, −3) are two vertices of a scalene triangle. Find two different coordinates for the third vertex.

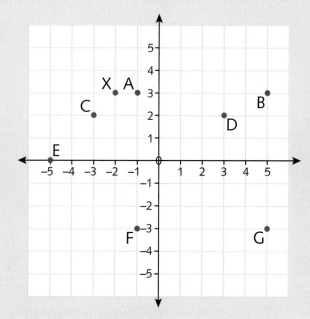

Plotting shapes in the four quadrants (1)

Plot, draw and label shapes in the four quadrants and predict missing coordinates

Challenge 1

Use Resource 12: 4-quadrant coordinate grids.

You will need:
- copies of Resource 12: 4-quadrant coordinate grids
- ruler

1 Plot these points on one of the grids.

A (4, 4)	B (−3, 3)
C (2, 3)	D (−5, 2)
E (−4, 0)	F (−3, −2)
G (2, −2)	H (0, −3)

2 Write the letter of the point or points that are:

    a in the 2nd quadrant   **b** in the 3rd quadrant

    c in the 4th quadrant   **d** on the x-axis   **e** on the y-axis

3 Using a ruler, join the points B, C, G and F in order to form a square.

Challenge 2

For each diagram, use a different grid on Resource 12: 4-quadrant coordinate grids.

1 On four separate grids, plot each point and join the points in order:

    a rectangle ABCD:
        A (−2, 3), B (3, 3),
        C (3, −4), D (−2, −4)

    b square EFGH:
        E (1, 3), F (5, −1),
        G (1, −5), H (−3, −1)

    c parallelogram IJKL:
        I (−3, 2), J (5, 2),
        K (3, −3), L (−5, −3)

    d rhombus PQRS:
        P (0, 0), Q (4, −2),
        R (0, −4), S (−4, −2)

2 The points T (−3, 3), U (3, 2) and V (2, −4) are three vertices of a square.

    • Plot the points and join them in order, T to U and U to V.

    • Find the coordinates of the missing vertex W.

    • Complete the drawing of the square.

3 The points A (−5, −1), B (1, 5) and C (5, 1)
are three vertices of a rectangle.

- Plot the points and join them in order, A to B and B to C.

- Find the coordinates of the missing vertex D.

- Complete the drawing of the rectangle.

4 The points E (3, 4), F (3, −3) and G (−3, −5)
are three vertices of a parallelogram.

- Plot the points and join them in order, E to F and F to G.

- Find the coordinates of the missing vertex H.

- Complete the drawing of the parallelogram.

5 The points J (−1, 3), K (1, 0) and L (−1, −3)
are three vertices of a rhombus.

- Plot the points and join them in order, J to K and K to L.

- Find the coordinates of the missing vertex M.

- Complete the drawing of the rhombus.

For each diagram, use a different grid on Resource 12:
4-quadrant coordinate grids.

1 AB is one side of a square ABCD, with A (0, −1) and B (4, −1).

- Plot the points A and B.

- Find two sets of coordinates for the missing vertices C and D.

- Complete the drawings of the squares.

2 FH is a diagonal of a square EFGH, with F (2, 3) and H (−4, −3).

- Plot the points F and H.

- Find the coordinates for the missing vertices E and G.

- Complete the drawing of the square.

Using coordinates to translate shapes (1)

Use coordinates to translate shapes into all four quadrants

For each grid, write the translation of
shape A to shape B.

Example

2 squares left, 3 squares down

Grid 1

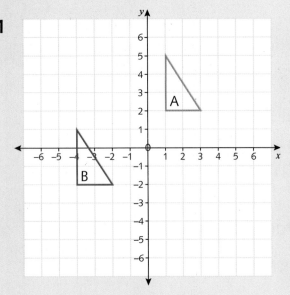

Grid 2

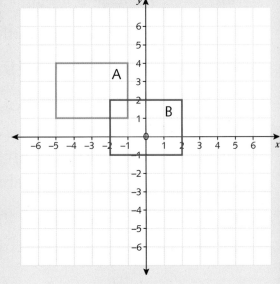

Grid 3

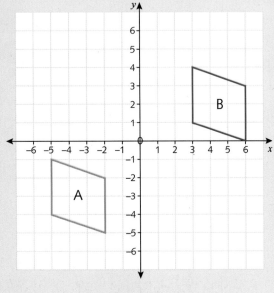

Grid 4

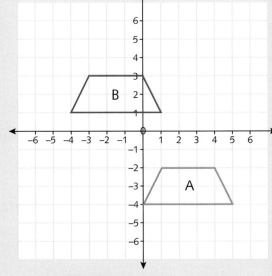

1 Copy each green shape A in Grids 1 to 4 of
Challenge 1 onto four different grids on
Resource 12: 4-quadrant coordinate grids.

You will need:
• copies of Resource 12:
  4-quadrant coordinate grids
• ruler
• green coloured pencil

For each one, translate shape A, as described below, to form shape B.

- **Grid 1:** 2 squares left, 3 squares down
- **Grid 2:** 6 squares right, 2 squares down
- **Grid 3:** 4 squares right, 3 squares up
- **Grid 4:** 1 square left, 6 squares up

2 Copy shapes A, B and C onto a grid on Resource 12: 4-quadrant coordinate grids.

Shape	x-coordinate	y-coordinate
A	−3	4
B	−1	2
C	1	0
D		

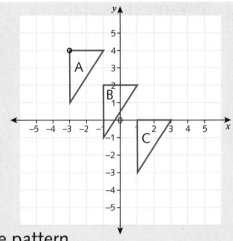

- The table shows the coordinates for the corresponding vertices for shapes A, B and C. Copy and complete the table giving the corresponding vertex for shape D by following the pattern.
- Draw shape D on the grid.

3 Copy the shapes D, E and F onto a grid on Resource 12: 4-quadrant coordinate grids.

Shape	x-coordinate	y-coordinate
D	−5	−3
E		
F		
G		

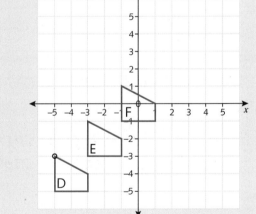

- Copy the table and fill in the corresponding vertices for shapes E and F.
- Work out and record the corresponding vertex for shape G by following the pattern.
- Draw shape G on the grid.

e

1 Design a different translating pattern for the trapezium in Challenge 2, Question 3 and draw three translations of the shape on a grid on Resource 12: 4-quadrant coordinate grids.

2 Choose a corresponding vertex for each shape and write their coordinates in a table.

3 Draw the next translation of the shape on the grid.

You will need:
- Resource 12: 4-quadrant coordinate grids
- ruler

Using coordinates to reflect shapes

Use coordinates to reflect shapes into all four quadrants

Challenge 1

1 Write the coordinates of each point and its image when reflected in the y-axis.

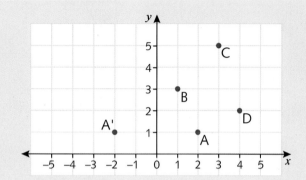

You will need:
- Resource 13: 2-quadrant coordinate grids
- ruler

Example

A (2, 1)   A' (−2, 1)

2 Copy each shape onto a different grid on Resource 13: 2-quadrant coordinate grids. Reflect each shape in the y-axis.

a

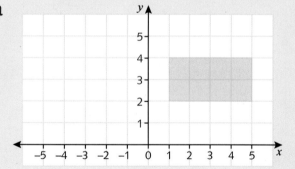

b

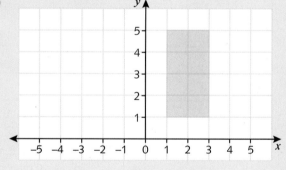

Challenge 2

1 Write the coordinates of each point and its image when reflected in the x-axis.

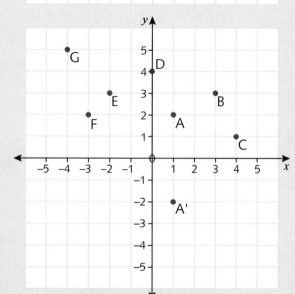

Example

A (1, 2)   A' (1, −2)

2 Copy each shape from the grids below onto a different grid on Resource 12: 4-quadrant coordinate grids.

For both Grids 1 and 2, draw the reflection of the shape in the y-axis and in the x-axis and write the coordinates for the vertices and their images.

You will need:
- Resource 12: 4-quadrant coordinate grids
- ruler

Grid 1

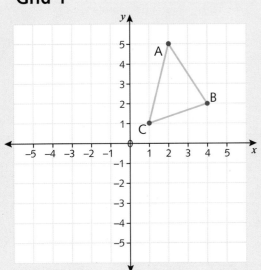

Grid 2

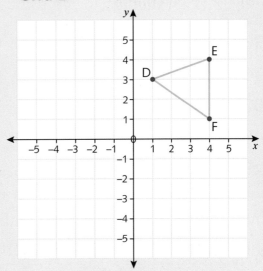

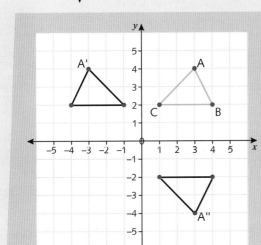

Example

A (3, 4), A' (−3, 4), A" (3, −4)

B (4, 2), B' (−4, 2), B" (4, −2)

C (1, 2), C'(−1, 2), C"(1, −2)

Draw a triangle with vertices P (0, 2), Q (4, 5) and R (3, 1) on Resource 12: 4-quadrant coordinate grids.

You will need:
- Resource 12: 4-quadrant coordinate grids
- ruler

a Reflect the triangle in the y-axis and write the coordinates of P', Q' and R'.

b Reflect the triangle in the x-axis and write the coordinates of P", Q" and R".

Written addition

- Add whole numbers using the formal written method of columnar addition
- Estimate and check the answer to a calculation

Challenge 1

Work out these calculations.

a   362 185 + 153 704
b   415 721 + 347 534
c   561 942 + 473 248
d   628 653 + 306 729
e   525 285 + 247 907
f   274 924 + 586 058
g   483 517 + 494 725
h   638 364 + 257 851
i   296 342 + 631 729
j   472 348 + 529 885

Example

```
  361 258
+ 636 581
  997 839
        1
```

Challenge 2

1 Estimate the answer to each calculation, then work it out.

a   3 762 485 + 1 229 152
b   2 383 962 + 2 652 725
c   4 296 422 + 3 487 384
d   2 762 471 + 4 083 982
e   4 282 692 + 3 815 854
f   6 385 352 + 2 563 983
g   3 592 284 + 5 835 799
h   5 836 365 + 3 927 289
i   2 973 483 + 605 863
j   716 493 + 3 853 632
k   67 892 + 1 360 542
l   4 396 387 + 728 195
m   6 396 293 + 45 829
n   768 219 + 6 926 103

2 Using the digits on the number cards, complete the calculation so that the answer is the highest possible number. The digits in each column must be different. Use trial and improvement to get the highest answer you can.

3 Using the same digits, make the lowest possible answer. Remember to use trial and improvement to get the lowest answer you can.

52

1 Estimate the answer to each calculation, then work it out.

a   6734 + 742 984 + 2 386 281

b   34 825 + 4 254 106 + 3762

c   23 876 + 58 108 + 2 782 354

d   5 387 205 + 38 298 + 599 486

e   3 293 382 + 617 296 + 4 286 125

f   687 462 + 836 277 + 4 275 196

g   383 582 + 9 607 306 + 1933

h   61 012 + 426 719 + 2 808 911

Example
2 365 256
851 734
+   65 726
3 282 716
1 1 1 1   1 1

2 Work out the missing numbers in these calculations.

a   3 872 386 + _____ = 5 803 862

b   872 492 + _____ = 2 764 821

c   3 297 378 + _____ = 5 545 503

d   2 764 297 + _____ = 4 723 285

e   876 955 + _____ = 3 608 275

f   75 316 + 483 592 + _____ = 2 685 273

g   650 732 + 1 487 284 + _____ = 4 217 639

h   782 916 + 2 935 272 + _____ = 5 074 286

i   615 109 + _____ + 1 696 500 = 9 809 205

j   974 486 + _____ + 40 792 = 3 084 817

Written subtraction

- Subtract whole numbers using the formal written method of columnar subtraction
- Estimate and check the answer to a calculation

Challenge 1

Work out these calculations.

a 573 296 – 281 542   b 427 386 – 193 228

c 632 492 – 307 915   d 426 145 – 281 630

e 574 851 – 327 188   f 803 274 – 351 748

g 956 062 – 672 391   h 944 264 – 587 093

i 893 216 – 775 608   j 816 749 – 652 871

Challenge 2

1 Estimate the answer to each calculation, then work it out.

a 5 487 287 – 3 429 159   b 4 252 961 – 2 504 315

c 7 289 242 – 3 739 625   d 6 029 882 – 2 415 945

e 9 401 194 – 4 721 638   f 8 339 327 – 1 728 543

g 7 284 191 – 5 471 654   h 9 386 194 – 5 847 528

i 4 296 252 – 735 298   j 5 825 261 – 563 865

k 638 194 – 8369   l 3 296 285 – 9673

m 2 384 901 – 863 552   n 836 285 – 89 644

o 7 291 304 – 862 899   p 6 928 362 – 725 633

q 8 296 235 – 9727   r 9 007 296 – 451 167

Example

$$
\begin{array}{r}
\overset{5\ 13}{2\ 6\overset{}{3}\ 6}\ \overset{7\ 11}{5\ 8\overset{}{1}} \\
-\ \ 3\ 6\ 1\ 2\ 5\ 8 \\
\hline
2\ 2\ 7\ 5\ 3\ 2\ 3
\end{array}
$$

2 Look at the following set of subtraction calculations. Think carefully about how you are going to use the formal written method of subtraction to work out the answers to these calculations.

a   5 872 130 – 2 874 274 – 674 923

b   7 394 866 – 538 744 – 2 651 908

c   6 458 428 – 2 649 106 – 9533

d   4 936 282 – 3 371 627 – 1 386 395

e   7 635 863 – 2 863 364 – 3 654 399

f   8 362 392 – 584 274 – 4 722 564

g   7 100 285 – 1 783 551 – 741 302

h   3 651 299 – 376 297 – 486 555

i   9 715 351 – 4 726 337 – 3 075 283

j   8 247 561 – 9999 – 3 762 286

Work out the missing numbers in these calculations.

a   6 397 282 – ⬚ = 4 276 295

b   5 207 466 – ⬚ = 1 542 396

c   4 296 385 – ⬚ = 2 524 719

d   3 829 603 – ⬚ = 2 657 843

e   8 602 552 – ⬚ = 864 971

f   ⬚ – 2 864 296 = 4 872 381

g   ⬚ – 378 272 = 3 981 228

h   ⬚ – 1 872 398 = 4 882 396

i   ⬚ – 9762 = 8 376 281

j   ⬚ – 801 362 = 7 449 276

Adding and subtracting decimals

Add and subtract decimals using the formal written methods of columnar addition and subtraction

Work out these calculations.

a 3874·48 + 4153·35

b 5247·27 + 3164·43

c 2914·56 + 4253·21

d 3225·37 + 2834·91

e 7625·28 − 3714·16

f 8364·36 − 5295·29

g 6268·65 − 2173·72

h 9467·78 − 5831·95

Example

```
  6581·57
+ 1258·44
---------
  7840·01
  1 11  1
```

1 Work out these calculations.

a 63 326·58 + 31 461·71

b 52 461·62 + 43 315·53

c 61 352·48 + 27 632·92

d 83 479·24 + 15 380·93

e 48 252·64 + 37 463·78

f 59 361·72 + 63 482·52

g 86 452·83 − 59 261·91

h 74 375·03 − 25 614·65

Example

```
  7 10 6 15  11
  8 0 7 6 · 1 9
− 5 4 5 6 · 4 2
---------------
  2 6 1 9 · 7 7
```

2 Play this addition game in a group of 2–4 players.

- Each player shuffles their cards and lays out ten each.
- Then, using the decimal point cards, players place their cards in this arrangement:

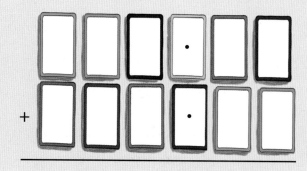

You will need:
- two sets 0–9 cards per player
- three decimal point cards per player
- pencil
- paper
- about 20 counters per group

- Players then work out the answer to their calculation.
- The winner of each round is the player with the highest total, and that player collects a counter.
- The overall winner is the player with most counters after six rounds.

3 Play this subtraction game in a group of 2–4 players.

- Each player shuffles their cards and lays out ten each.
- Then, using their the decimal point cards, players place their cards in this arrangement:

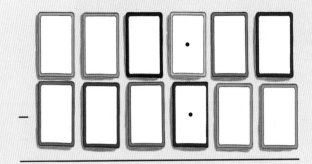

- Players then work out the answer to their calculation.
- The winner of each round is the player with the smallest answer, and that player collects a counter.
- The overall winner is the player with most counters after six rounds.

1 Work out these calculations.

a 2487·46 + 27 826·3   b 45 272·72 − 3962·8

c 52 835·35 + 286 486·62   d 731 362·5 + 67 251·2

e 65 972·98 − 42 252·382   f 82 616·3 − 5826·296

2 These numbers are the answers. Write one addition and one subtraction calculation for each answer. The calculations must be 8-digit to 2 decimal places plus/minus 8-digit to 2 decimal places.

> **Hint**
>
> Use the inverse operation!

a 462 712·53   b 504 724·62   c 826 507·11

d 483 566·72   e 638 931·63   f 3 847 116·83

Book problems

- Solve multi-step problems, deciding which operations and methods to use and why
- Use estimation to check accuracy of answers

The tables below show the bestselling books of all time.

Bestselling books 1–10		
Position	Type of book	Total sales
1st	mystery novel	5 094 805
2nd	children's	4 475 152
3rd	children's	4 200 654
4th	children's	4 179 479
5th	novel	3 758 936
6th	children's	3 583 215
7th	children's	3 484 047
8th	children's	3 377 906
9th	mystery novel	3 193 346
10th	children's	2 950 264

Bestselling books 90–100		
Position	Type of book	Total sales
90th	science	816 907
91st	comic annual	816 585
92nd	novel	815 586
93rd	novel	814 370
94th	novel	809 641
95th	novel	808 311
96th	novel	807 311
97th	cookery	794 201
98th	novel	792 187
99th	autobiography	791 507
100th	cookery	791 095

Challenge
1

Answer these problems.

a What is the difference in sales between the 92nd most popular book and the 97th most popular book?

b What are the total sales for both cookery books?

c Josh buys a cookery book and a novel. He pays €38. Salma buys the same cookery book and two copies of the same novel as Josh. She pays €45. What is the price of the cookery book?

d If the autobiography sells a further 32 000 copies in shops and 43 000 copies online, what would be the total sales?

Answer these problems.

a The total sales for the top two bestselling children's books is 8 675 806. The total sales for hardback books was 3 400 000. Book One sold 2 500 000 copies in hardback. Book Two sold 3 300 654 copies in paperback. How many copies of Book Two were sold in hardback? How many copies of Book One were sold in paperback?

b The price of the bestselling children's novel was €7 at the local shop. A bookshop allocated €8450 to spend on copies of the novel. They ordered as many copies as they could afford. How much money was left over?

c Peter buys the latest cookery book and four novels. He pays €50.50. Jackie buys two copies of the same cookery book and two novels. She pays €56. What is the price of one novel?

d Josh rounds the sales of two of the books and adds them together. His answer is 1 618 000. Which two books' sales did he round?

e Salma finds the difference between the sales of two books from the top ten. Her answer was 381 030. Which two books did she choose?

1 Answer these problems.

a Three friends go into the bookshop. Billy buys a mystery novel and a science book. He pays €19.94. Gemma buys the same science book and an atlas. Her bill comes to €28.98. Louis buys the mystery novel and the atlas and pays €24.94. What is the price of each book?

b The publisher ordered more copies of its two bestsellers, a novel and a cookery book, to be printed. The novel was packed in crates of 10 000 and the cookery book, as it was larger, was packed in crates of 3000.

If 210 000 copies of each book were printed, how many more crates of cookery books were there than novels?

c What were the total sales of the three most popular children's books?

d The author of the bestselling detective novel signed approximately 12 700 copies of his book. The author of the bestselling children's book managed to sign more of her books, and 4 461 152 copies were sold unsigned. What was the total number of signed books sold?

2 Write a challenging word problem using the information in the table and give it to your partner to work out.

Numbers with 3 decimal places

Identify the value of each digit in a number with 3 decimal places

Challenge 1

1 Count on five numbers from each number with 2 decimal places.

Example

6·38 , 6·39, 6·40, 6·41, 6·42, 6·43

a 3·47 b 2·89 c 4·07 d 5·26 e 3·98 f 4·57

g 6·39 h 2·06 i 8·18 j 4·95 k 7·35 l 8·88

2 Look at the decimal numbers in Question 1. What two numbers with 1 decimal place do they come between?

Example

6·3, 6·38 , 6·4

Hint
Convert the tenths into hundredths,
6·3 to 6·30 and 6·4 to 6·40.

Challenge 2

1 Count on five numbers from each number with 3 decimal places.

Example

6·328 , 6·329, 6·330, 6·331, 6·332, 6·333

a 3·867 b 6·108 c 2·759 d 9·015 e 4·268 f 7·009

g 5·486 h 3·111 i 5·437 j 6·546 k 1·001 l 4·873

2 Look at the decimal numbers in Question 1. What two numbers with 2 decimal places do they come between?

Example

6·32, 6·328 , 6·33

Hint
Convert the hundredths into thousandths,
6·32 to 6·320 and 6·33 to 6·330.

3 Choose five numbers from Question 1 and write the value of each of the digits.

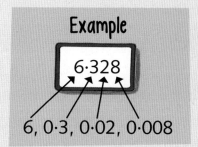

Example

6·328

6, 0·3, 0·02, 0·008

4 Put all the numbers from Question 1 in order, smallest to largest.

5 Write ten numbers with 3 decimal places where:

- the thousandths digit is even
- the hundredths digit is lower than 5
- the tenths digit is half the thousandths digit.

3·428 fits all these properties.

1 Use these four number cards.

5   9   2   7

a Make twelve different numbers with a 1s digit and 3 decimal places.

b Write the numbers in order, smallest to largest, leaving a space in between each of the numbers.

Example

2·579, ☐ , 2·597, ☐ , 5·279 …

c Write numbers with 3 decimal places that could come in between your numbers and keep the order.

2 Write a number with 3 decimal places that could come between each pair of decimals.

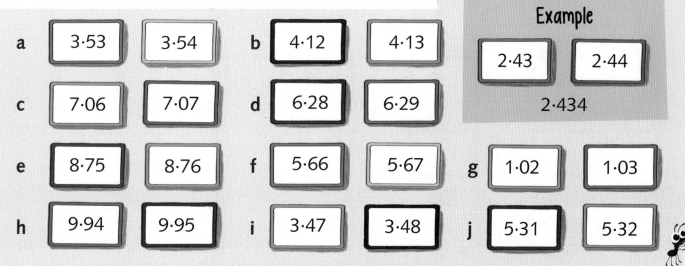

a 3·53   3·54   **b** 4·12   4·13

Example

2·43   2·44

c 7·06   7·07   **d** 6·28   6·29

2·434

e 8·75   8·76   **f** 5·66   5·67   **g** 1·02   1·03

h 9·94   9·95   **i** 3·47   3·48   **j** 5·31   5·32

Multiplying and dividing by 10, 100 and 1000

Multiply and divide numbers by 10, 100 and 1000 where the answers are up to 3 decimal places

Challenge 1

1 Use Resource 15: 10, 100 spinner. For each number below, spin the spinner and carry out the operation it lands on.

You will need:
- Resource 15: 10, 100 spinner
- paper clip and pencil – for the spinner

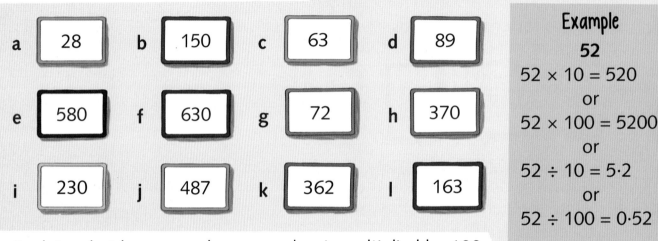

a	28	b	150	c	63	d	89
e	580	f	630	g	72	h	370
i	230	j	487	k	362	l	163

Example
52
52 × 10 = 520
or
52 × 100 = 5200
or
52 ÷ 10 = 5·2
or
52 ÷ 100 = 0·52

2 Explain what happens when a number is multiplied by 100.

3 Explain what happens when a number is divided by 10.

Challenge 2

1 Use Resource 16: 10, 100, 1000 spinner. For each number below, spin the spinner and carry out the operation it lands on.

You will need:
- Resource 16: 10, 100, 1000 spinner
- paper clip and pencil – for the spinner

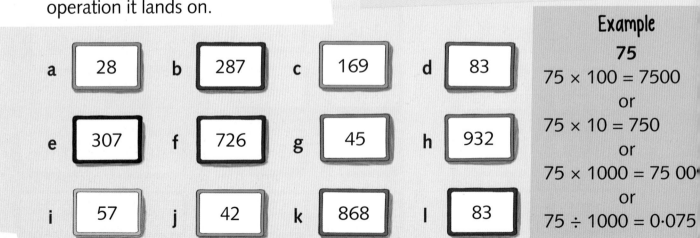

a	28	b	287	c	169	d	83
e	307	f	726	g	45	h	932
i	57	j	42	k	868	l	83

Example
75
75 × 100 = 7500
or
75 × 10 = 750
or
75 × 1000 = 75 00*
or
75 ÷ 1000 = 0·075

2 Multiply and divide each decimal number by 100.

a	36·2	**b**	83·6	**c**	92·5
d	73·1	**e**	43·7	**f**	63·2
g	92·9	**h**	28·3	**i**	82·7

Example
46·8
46·8 × 100 = 4680
46·8 ÷ 100 = 0·468

3 Play this game with a partner. Use Resource 16: 10, 100, 1000 spinner.

- Choose a 2-digit start number and both write it down.
- Take turns to spin the spinner.
- Carry out the operation it lands on with your start number.
- Write your answer underneath your start number. This answer becomes your new start number.
- The winner is the player with the highest number after ten turns each.

1 Use Resource 16: 10, 100, 1000 spinner. For each number, spin the spinner and carry out the operation it lands on.

You will need:
- Resource 16: 10, 100, 1000 spinner
- paper clip and pencil – for the spinner

a 1836	**b** 2924		
c 3715	**d** 5206		

Example
25 486
25 486 × 1000 = 25 486 000
25 486 ÷ 1000 = 25·486

e 7188	**f** 34 492	**g** 87 725	**h** 21 396
i 50 532	**j** 47 872	**k** 19 294	**l** 74 816

2 The supermarket orders many items in boxes of 100. They have just received the delivery below. How many of each item do they have?

- 36 boxes of dog food
- 260 boxes of cereal
- 198 boxes of biscuits

- 86·5 boxes of jam
  (One box got dropped on the way and half the jars were broken!)

3 Using Resource 16: 10, 100, 1000 spinner, design a game to practise multiplying and dividing by 10, 100 and 1000.

Multiplying decimals

Multiply decimals by whole numbers including in practical contexts

Challenge 1

1 Copy and complete these decimal 'times tables'.

a
1 × 0·2 = 0·2
2 × 0·2 = 0·4
3 × 0·2 = 0·6
4 × 0·2 = 0·8
5 × 0·2 =
6 × 0·2 =
7 × 0·2 =
8 × 0·2 =
9 × 0·2 =
10 × 0·2 =
11 × 0·2 =
12 × 0·2 =

b
1 × 0·3 = 0·3
2 × 0·3 = 0·6
3 × 0·3 = 0·9
4 × 0·3 = 1·2
5 × 0·3 =
6 × 0·3 =
7 × 0·3 =
8 × 0·3 =
9 × 0·3 =
10 × 0·3 =
11 × 0·3 =
12 × 0·3 =

c
1 × 0·5 = 0·5
2 × 0·5 = 1·0
3 × 0·5 = 1·5
4 × 0·5 = 2·0
5 × 0·5 =
6 × 0·5 =
7 × 0·5 =
8 × 0·5 =
9 × 0·5 =
10 × 0·5 =
11 × 0·5 =
12 × 0·5 =

2 Work out each calculation. In brackets, write the times table fact that helps you work it out.

Example

0·4 × 3 = 1·2 (4 × 3 = 12)

a 0·4 × 2　**b** 0·4 × 5　**c** 0·6 × 2

d 0·6 × 4　**e** 0·7 × 5　**f** 0·8 × 3

Challenge 2

1 Copy and complete these decimal 'times tables'.

1 × 0·6 = 0·6　　2 × 0·6 = 1·2　　3 × 0·6 =
4 × 0·6 =　　5 × 0·6 =　　6 × 0·6 =
7 × 0·6 =　　8 × 0·6 =　　9 × 0·6 =
10 × 0·6 =　　11 × 0·6 =　　12 × 0·6 =

2 Which 'decimal × whole number' calculations will these multiplication facts help you work out?

> **Example**
> Multiplication fact: 3 × 4 = 12
> 0·3 × 4 = 1·2
> 3 × 0·4 = 1·2

a   5 × 3   b   4 × 7   c   2 × 8   d   6 × 3   e   8 × 4

f   7 × 6   g   3 × 9   h   5 × 6   i   8 × 9   j   7 × 7

3 Work out the cost of these items. Show your working.

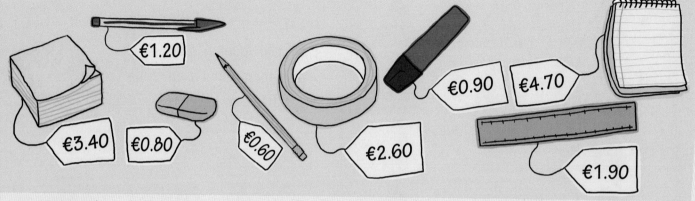

a   6 pencils   b   8 erasers   c   13 highlighter pens

d   4 sticky note pads   e   7 rulers   f   15 pens and 7 erasers

g   12 rolls of sticky tape h   5 notebooks   i   13 rulers and 20 pencils

1 Copy and complete this bill from the hardware shop.

Item	Price per metre	Number of metres	Calculation	Total price
string	€0.70	24		
rope	€0.90	31		
leather	€4	15·6		
fine wire	€2.30	27		
nylon rope	€0.40	43		
thick wire	€2.70	35		
chain	€3.20	40		

2 Stan goes to the hardware shop. He has €20 to spend.
How many metres of string can he buy? How much change will he get?

3 William has €30 to spend. He wants to buy a combination of rope and fine wire. He needs more rope than wire. He wants to spend as much of his money as he can. What should he buy?

Rounding decimals

Solve problems which require answers to be rounded to specified degrees of accuracy

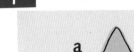 **1** Round these decimals to the nearest whole number.

a 4·6   **b** 2·8   **c** 7·3

d 9·5   **e** 1·4   **f** 3·6

g 8·8   **h** 3·2   **i** 8·4

j 5·1   **k** 8·8   **l** 9·1   **m** 7·5   **n** 2·6

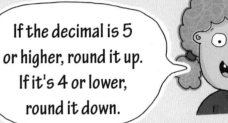

If the decimal is 5 or higher, round it up. If it's 4 or lower, round it down.

2 Write five decimal numbers that would round to each of these numbers.

a 5   **b** 7   **c** 3   **d** 4   **e** 10

Challenge 2

1 Round these decimals to the nearest whole number.

a 35·7   **b** 28·62   **c** 49·5   **d** 26·32

e 41·74   **f** 50·4   **g** 18·61   **h** 63·49   **i** 28·17

j 83·1   **k** 47·39   **l** 72·88   **m** 17·99   **n** 56·5

Example
36·7 rounds to 37
35·79 rounds to 36

2 Round all the numbers with 2 decimal places from Question 1 to the nearest tenth.

3 Write five decimals that would round to each of these tenths.

a 6·2   **b** 2·9   **c** 1·4   **d** 5·7   **e** 9·1   **f** 3·6

4 For each of these measurements, write down a time when:

- the exact measurement would be best
- the measurement rounded to the nearest tenth would be best
- the measurement rounded to the nearest whole number would be best.

Explain your reasons.

a Sophie is 1·45 metres tall.

b The hall is 35·82 metres long.

c A book costs €4.85.

d The recipe says '0·75 kg of flour'.

e The tree is 11·25 metres tall.

f The distance from home to school is 4·37 km.

g The dog weighs 6·98 kg.

h The play lasts 2·5 hours.

1 Round these decimals to the nearest whole number.

a	37·963	b	26·286	c	39·301	d	48·199	e	93·832
f	25·726	g	49·075	h	35·542	i	95·478	j	86·501
k	68·383	l	74·307	m	49·968	n	56·535	o	27·455

2 Choose five decimals from Question 1 and round each number to the nearest tenth.

3 Choose five different decimals from Question 1 and round each number to the nearest hundredth.

4 Jemima says, "When I go to the supermarket, I estimate my total bill this way: whenever I put anything in the trolley, I round it to the nearest euro."

a Write a shopping bill with prices of ten items where her system would work.

b Write another shopping bill with prices of ten items where it would not work.

c Overall, do you think Jemima's system is a good one? Explain your answer.

Converting units of length

Convert from smaller to larger units of length using decimal notation

Challenge 1

1 Write each length in centimetres using decimals.

    a 6 cm 3 mm   **b** 12 cm 9 mm   **c** 75 mm   **d** 148 mm

2 Write each length in metres using decimals.

    a 14 m 39 cm   **b** 52 m 60 cm   **c** 827 cm   **d** 309 cm

3 Write each length in kilometres using decimals.

    a 8 km 600 m   **b** 4 km 130 m   **c** 6500 m   **d** 7720 m

Challenge 2

1 Write each length in kilometres.

    a 3727 m   **b** 4420 m   **c** 5010 m   **d** 3205 m

2 Write each length in metres.

    a 0·725 km   **b** 0·408 km   **c** 914 cm   **d** 702 cm

3 Write each length in centimetres then order the lengths, longest to shortest.

    a 66 mm   **b** 242 mm   **c** 1·6 m   **d** 9·73 m

4 The carpenter has cut some strips of wood.

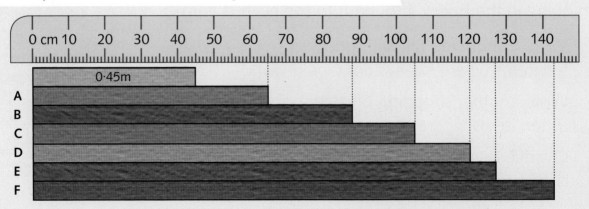

a Write the length of each strip of wood in metres.

b Find the difference in length in centimetres between these strips of wood.

    i A and D   **ii** B and E   **iii** C and F

c Find the total length in metres of these strips of wood.

    i A and E   **ii** B and F   **iii** C and B   **iv** D and F

d How many metres long is each small piece of wood when:

    i strip C is cut into 5 equal lengths?

    ii strip D is cut into 8 equal lengths?

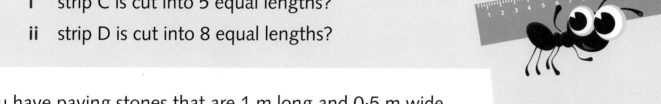

e You have paving stones that are 1 m long and 0·5 m wide. How many different arrangements of paving stones can you make for 1 m wide paths that are 2 m, 2·5 m and 3 m long? Begin as shown in the Example.

You will need:
- 1 cm square dot paper

Example

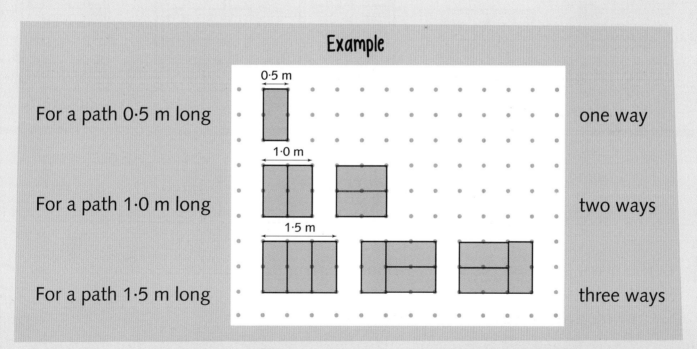

For a path 0·5 m long		one way
For a path 1·0 m long		two ways
For a path 1·5 m long		three ways

a Draw the paths on 1 cm square dot paper until you see a pattern.

b Write in words how the pattern works.

Hint

The answer for a path 2·0 m long is not four ways!

c If the path was 5 m long, how many different arrangements of paving stones could you make? Investigate.

Sporting distances

Convert between units of length to solve problems using decimal notation

Challenge 1

1 The cricket ground is overlooked by five blocks of flats. Work out the height of each block of flats.

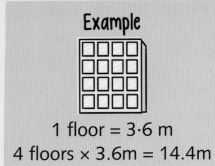

Example

1 floor = 3·6 m
4 floors × 3.6m = 14.4m

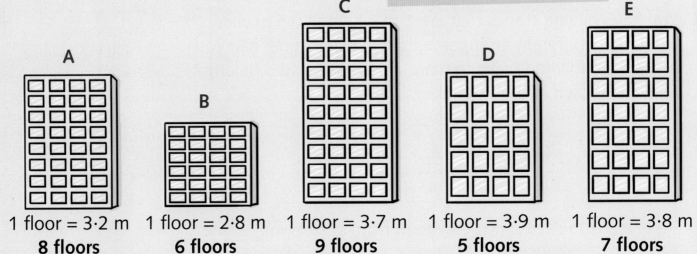

A
1 floor = 3·2 m
8 floors

B
1 floor = 2·8 m
6 floors

C
1 floor = 3·7 m
9 floors

D
1 floor = 3·9 m
5 floors

E
1 floor = 3·8 m
7 floors

2 How many metres taller is block C than:

    a block B?   **b** block D?

Challenge 2

1 The distance round the sports ground running track is 420 m. Colin runs nine times round the track in training. How far does he run in kilometres?

2 Winston is a distance runner and he runs the same route every time. In five evenings, he ran a total of 4·73 km. How long is his training route:

    a in kilometres?   **b** in metres?

3 Meg cycles 37·5 km from home to school and home again in one week. How far is her house from her school?

4 The table shows the results of a long jump competition. By how many centimetres did Jordan beat each of his competitors?

Name	Jordan	Keira	Len	Mark	Naomi
Length of jump (m)	4·42	3·97	4·29	3·88	4·16

5 A cross-country cycle competition has races at six different venues in Britain. Find the total length of each race in kilometres.

	Venue	Length of one course lap (km)	Number of laps
a	Peak District	3·87	4
b	Borders	2·85	5
c	Lake District	4·19	4
d	North Wales	5·025	3
e	South Downs	2·64	5
f	East Anglia	3·78	4

Sheena has to cut lengths of ribbon from a 32 m roll for the medals that the winners will receive at the school's sports day. She has mislaid her measuring tape and does the following:

- unrolls the ribbon, folds it in half and cuts it
- folds each piece in half and cuts it
- folds each of the four pieces in half and cuts them.

a How many pieces of ribbon will she have if she continues to fold and cut the ribbon a further three times?

b What is the final length of each piece of ribbon?

Hint

Making a table similar to this one will help organise your answer.

Number of folds	0	1	2	3
Number of pieces of ribbon	1	2	4	
Length of each piece of ribbon (m)	32	16	8	

The Kelly family go to the circus

Convert between units of length to solve problems using decimal notation

Challenge 1

This photograph of the Kelly children is for Gran. Alex wrote each of their heights underneath the photo so that Gran could see how tall they all were.

Alex 1·51 m Bob 1·25 m Chris 1·39 m Derek 1·44 m Ellen 96 cm

1 Find in metres the difference in height between:

  a Alex and Bob
  b Alex and Chris
  c Alex and Derek
  d Alex and Ellen

2 Find, in centimetres, the difference between the tallest and the shortest child.

3 Who is 14 cm taller than Bob?

Challenge 2

1 The Kelly family have tickets for the circus in town. They travel 4·375 km by car to the station, 36·83 km by train to town and walk 50 m to the circus.

  a How many kilometres do they travel altogether by car, there and back?

  b How many kilometres is the round trip to and from the circus?

2 The tightrope wire is 21 m from the ground. The rungs on the ladder from the ground to the tightrope platform are at 60 cm intervals. Angelino, the tightrope walker, has climbed to the 15th rung from the ground.

  a What is his height from the ground in metres?

  b How many metres has he still to climb to reach the tightrope platform?

3 Chris Kelly's footprint is 245 mm long. The clown who wears enormous shoes has a footprint 8 times as long. Find the length of the clown's footprint:

    a in centimetres   **b** in metres

4 The clown makes his own shoelaces.
Each lace is 85 cm long.

    a How many pairs of shoelaces can he make from a 10 m narrow strip of leather?

    b How many centimetres of leather will be left over?

5 Enrico needs some rope to tether the horses. He finds three lengths of rope in each of two boxes. If Enrico takes a length of rope from box A and joins it to one from box B, how many different lengths of combined rope can he make?

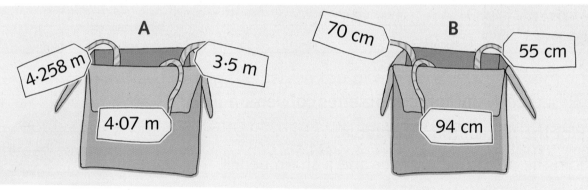

The circus clowns have to ring the bell on top of each box, starting from one end of the double row of boxes, and visiting each bell once only. The clowns may not take any diagonal paths between the bells. The plan shows the distance between each bell.

a Work out the shortest route that a clown could take to ring all the bells.

b Write this shortest distance in metres.

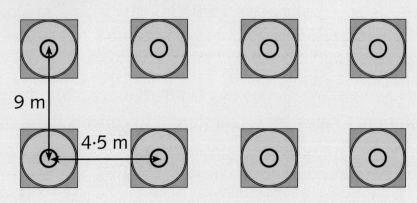

Converting miles to kilometres

Convert between miles and kilometres

You will need:
- Resource 17: Miles to kilometres conversion graph
- ruler

Challenges 1,2

1 Using the rule, copy and complete the table by converting miles to kilometres and using the distances to write the coordinates.

Rule
5 miles is approximately equal to 8 kilometres.

Miles	0	5	10	15	20	25
Kilometres	0	8				
Coordinates	(0, 0)	(5, 8)				

2 Use Resource 17: Miles to kilometres conversion graph.

- Plot the points from your table.
- Join the points with a ruler and a sharp pencil.
- Extend the straight line as far as it will go.

3 Use your graph from Question 2 to answer these questions.

a 16 km ≈ [   ] miles

b 40 km ≈ [   ] miles

c 15 miles ≈ [   ] km

d 30 miles ≈ [   ] km

≈ means 'approximately equal to'

Challenge 2

1 Use your graph from Challenge 1, Question 2 to convert these distances.

a 20 miles   b 35 miles   c 64 km

d 80 km   e 50 miles   f 60 miles

2 At point **a** on the straight line, 12 km converts to 7·5 miles.

Copy and complete for these points shown on the line.

Point	Kilometres	Miles
a	12	7·5
b	20	
c		
d		
e		

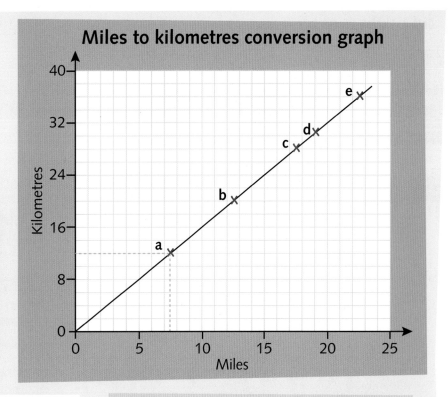

Miles to kilometres conversion graph

3 Convert these distances to kilometres.

  a 100 miles   **b** 250 miles

  c 450 miles   **d** 505 miles

Hint

If 5 miles converts to 8 kilometres, then 50 miles converts to 80 kilometres.

4 Convert these distances to miles.

  a 240 km   **b** 640 km   **c** 480 km   **d** 1000 km

5 For each distance, write which approximate conversion is sensible and explain why.

  a 70 miles ≈ 110 km or 45 km   **b** 150 km ≈ 240 miles or 90 miles

Two couples hired a camper van for their holiday in France.

- Stewart drove the van for 50% of the total distance.

- Stewart's wife Sheila drove half as far as the combined distance driven by the other couple.

- Jack drove four times as far as his wife Jenny.

- Jenny drove the van for 64 kilometres.

  a How many kilometres did each person drive?

  b What was the total distance driven, in miles, during their holiday in France?

Multiples and factors

Identify common factors and common multiples

Challenge 1

1 List the first six multiples of each of the numbers below. Then for each pair of numbers, circle the lowest common multiple.

a   6   9

b   12   18

c   7   4

d   10   25

e   21   14

f   30   50

g   15   20

h   5   8

2 Find all of the common multiples below 100 for each set of numbers.

a   6, 8   b   12, 15   c   4, 13   d   2, 8

Challenge 2

1 Write all of the factors of these sets of numbers. Find and circle the common factors of each set of numbers.

Example
16: ①, ②, ④, 8, 16
20: ①, ②, ④, 5, 10, 20

Hint
A factor is a whole number that divides exactly into another whole number.

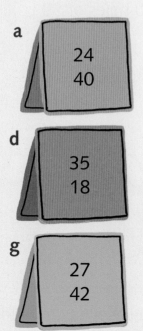

a
24
40

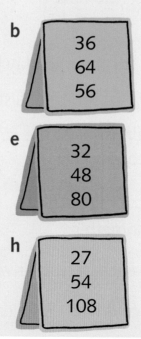

b
36
64
56

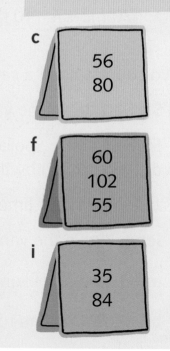

c
56
80

d
35
18

e
32
48
80

f
60
102
55

g
27
42

h
27
54
108

i
35
84

2 Write the highest common factor for each set of numbers in Question 1.

3 Find a number that has at least five common factors with each of these numbers.

    a 32   **b** 44   **c** 100

    d 16   **e** 81

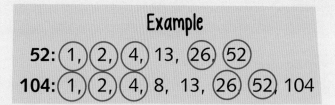

Example

52: (1) (2) (4) 13, (26) (52)

104: (1) (2) (4) 8, 13, (26) (52) 104

1 Find the prime factors of these numbers. Draw factor trees to help you.

a 87

b 232

c 185

d 98

e 146

f 356

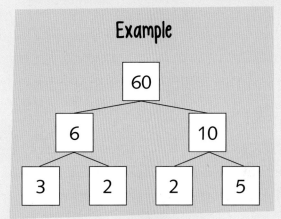

Example

60 → 6, 10
6 → 3, 2
10 → 2, 5

2 Describe a way of making sure you have found all of the factors of a number.

3 Copy and complete the table on the right.

- In the first column of the table write the numbers 1 to 12.

- In the second column, write any number that has that many factors.

- In the third column, write all the factors of this number.

Example

Number of factors	Number	Factors
1	1	1
2	2	1, 2
3	9	1, 3, 9
4		
5		
6		

Division ThHTO ÷ O with a remainder

- Use the formal written method of short division to calculate ThHTO ÷ O
- Estimate and check the answer to a calculation

Challenge 1

1 Find the multiple of 6 that comes immediately before each of these numbers.

(23) (61) (38) (53) (68) (47) (79) (85)

Example
16 → 12

2 Find the multiple of 8 that comes immediately before each of these numbers.

(27) (68) (55) (92) (34) (39) (83) (95)

Example
34 → 32

3 Find the multiple of 3 that comes immediately before each of these numbers.

(22) (17) (38) (62) (14) (28) (35) (92)

Example
10 → 9

4 Find the multiple of 7 that comes immediately before each of these numbers.

(79) (85) (23) (62) (54) (69) (85) (92)

Example
15 → 14

Challenge 2

For each division calculation, write your estimate, then use the formal written method of short division to work out the answer. Record any answers with a remainder as a decimal and then as a fraction.

Example

$2376 \div 5 \rightarrow 2500 \div 5 = 500$

$$\begin{array}{c} \text{Th} \quad \text{H} \quad \text{T} \quad \text{O} \cdot \text{t} \\ 4 \quad 7 \quad 5 \cdot 2 \text{ or } 475\frac{1}{5} \\ \hline 5\overline{)2\ 3\ ^3 7\ ^2 6 \cdot ^1 0} \end{array}$$

a 3598 ÷ 5

b 5277 ÷ 6

c 7645 ÷ 4

d 8664 ÷ 8

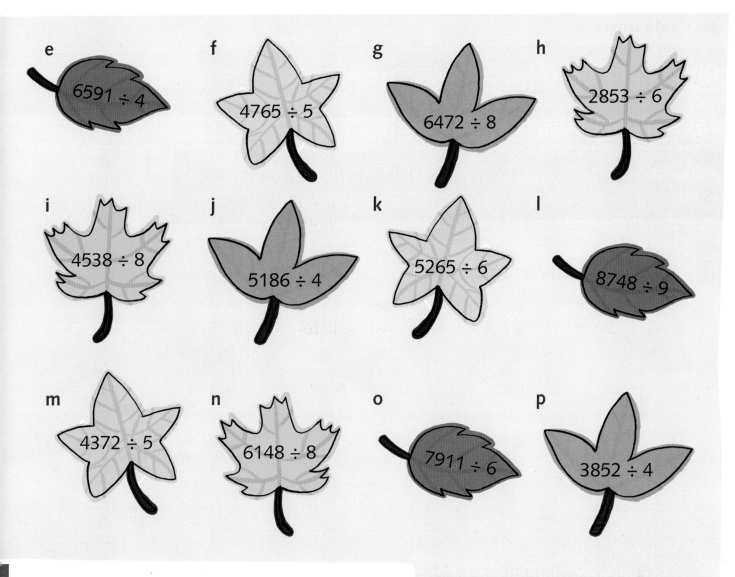

e 6591 ÷ 4

f 4765 ÷ 5

g 6472 ÷ 8

h 2853 ÷ 6

i 4538 ÷ 8

j 5186 ÷ 4

k 5265 ÷ 6

l 8748 ÷ 9

m 4372 ÷ 5

n 6148 ÷ 8

o 7911 ÷ 6

p 3852 ÷ 4

Write a calculation to match each instruction.

a Divide a 4-digit number by 6, to give an answer that includes a fraction remainder of $\frac{1}{2}$.

b Divide a 3-digit number by 9, to give an answer that includes a fraction remainder of $\frac{1}{3}$.

c Divide a 4-digit number by 5, to give an answer that ends in ·4.

d Divide a 4-digit number between 6000 and 7000 by 8, to give an answer that ends in ·75.

e Divide a 4-digit even number by 3 to give an answer that includes a fraction remainder of $\frac{2}{3}$.

Dividing ThHTO by 11 and 12 using the formal written method of short division

- Use the most efficient method to calculate ThHTO ÷ TO
- Estimate and check the answer to a calculation

1 Multiply each number by 11.

Example

7 × 11 = 77

a 9

b 11

c 200

d 60

e 8

f 12

g 40

h 500

i 30

j 700

2 Multiply each number by 12.

Example

5 × 12 = 60

a 7

b 20

c 400

d 6

e 8

f 120

g 100

h 50

i 300

j 9

3 Work these calculations out mentally.

a 720 ÷ 12	b 770 ÷ 11	c 990 ÷ 11	d 360 ÷ 12
e 3300 ÷ 11	f 6000 ÷ 12	g 4400 ÷ 11	h 9600 ÷ 12

1   Sort the calculations into two groups: those you would work out mentally and those where you would use a written method.

Then work out the answer to each calculation. For those calculations that need a written method, use the formal written method of short division.

Example

Th	H	T	O
	6	4	1

$12\overline{)7\ 6\ {}^49\ {}^12}$

a	432 ÷ 12	b	5160 ÷ 12	c	5566 ÷ 11	d	3768 ÷ 12
e	4741 ÷ 11	f	7183 ÷ 11	g	2880 ÷ 12	h	3564 ÷ 11
i	3696 ÷ 12	j	4872 ÷ 12	k	396 ÷ 11	l	8899 ÷ 11

2   Check the answer to each written calculation using the inverse method of multiplication.

1   Find the answers to these problems.

a   Eleven friends pay €2354 between them for their ski holiday. If each person pays the same amount, how much does each person pay?

b   The Jones family travel by car to their relatives. It takes them approximately 12 hours to complete the journey of 1380 km. On average, how many kilometres per hour did they travel?

c   James and William travel to Europe by car on business. They are away for 12 days and during this time travel a total of 3246 kilometres. On average, how far did they travel each day?

d   Sasha pays €6743 for an 11-day holiday. Jamal pays €6996 for a 12-day holiday. Who pays more per day for their holiday? How much more?

2   The answer is €503.25. What could the question be?

Solving word problems (2)

- Solve problems involving addition, subtraction, multiplication and division
- Estimate and check the answer to a calculation

Challenge 1

Look at the calculations either side of each box. Copy the calculations and use the symbol <, = or > to make each statement true.

a 631 ÷ 9 ____ 483 ÷ 4   b 148 ÷ 4 ____ 16 × 6

c 26 – 19 ____ 28 ÷ 4   d 642 ÷ 2 ____ 42 × 8

e 56 × 9 ____ 2624 ÷ 4   f 540 ÷ 6 ____ 20 × 7

g 69 + 18 ____ 648 ÷ 8   h 63 × 7 ____ 624 – 187

i 3535 ÷ 5 ____ 1000 – 293   j 1344 ÷ 6 ____ 14 × 16

Challenge 2

Find the answer to these problems.

Buffet breakfast	€11
Omelette	€7
Beans on toast	€6
Cereal	€5
Coffee	€3
Tea	€2

a The cafe specialises in making omelettes for breakfast. They have a total of 62 dozen eggs. If each omelette uses 3 eggs, how many omelettes can be made?

b At the end of the morning, the chef calculated that he had used 696 eggs for omelettes. How many dozen eggs is this? If he started with 62 dozen, how many eggs were not used?

c 756 cups of tea and 879 cups of coffee were sold in one week. How much money was taken?

d The total takings from buffet breakfasts for one week was €9086. How many buffet breakfasts were sold?

e In one week, 632 omelettes were sold and €4656 was taken for beans on toast. Which item was most popular?

f The cafe has a special offer: 'Buy 2 buffet breakfasts and receive your next one half price.' Joel uses this deal to buy breakfast every day for 3 weeks. What is his total spend?

g The takings for buffet breakfasts in one week were €5588. The following week, the takings increased to €8404. How many more breakfasts were sold in the second week?

h Martin buys breakfast every day of the week. He has a buffet breakfast at the weekend, beans on toast on a Monday, an omelette on Wednesday and Friday, and cereal on each of the other days. He buys a cup of tea each weekday and a coffee both days at the weekend. How much does he spend on breakfasts in a week?

Use the information on the menu board to write your own word problems. Write the calculation you would use and the answer on another piece of paper. Give your word problems to your partner to solve. Check that your partner's answers match yours.

Seafood salad	€12
Chicken salad sandwich	€11
Salad with garlic bread	€9
Soup	€6
French fries	€4
Cold drinks	€2.50
Hot drinks	€3

Fraction and decimal equivalents (1)

Associate a fraction with division and calculate decimal fraction equivalents

1 Copy each number line, then complete it choosing decimals from the number cards below. Some decimals will be used more than once.

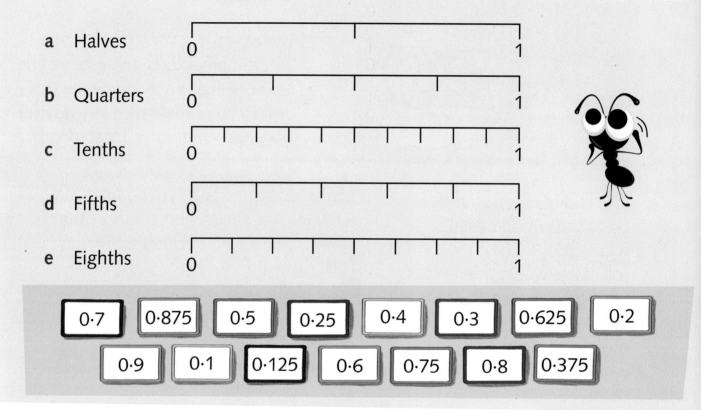

a Halves
b Quarters
c Tenths
d Fifths
e Eighths

Cards: 0·7 0·875 0·5 0·25 0·4 0·3 0·625 0·2
0·9 0·1 0·125 0·6 0·75 0·8 0·375

2 Complete the fraction wall on Resource 22: Fraction wall. What fractions are equivalent to the decimal fractions you have written? Try to remember all the equivalences and write them down.

You will need:
• Resource 22: Fraction wall

3 Copy and complete these calculations.

a 0·5 + ☐ = 1

b 0·25 + ☐ + ☐ + ☐ = 1

c 0·1 + 0·1 + ☐ + ☐ + ☐ + ☐ + ☐ + ☐ + ☐ + ☐ = 1

d 0·2 + ☐ + ☐ + ☐ + ☐ = 1

e 0·125 + 0·125 + ☐ + ☐ + ☐ + ☐ + ☐ + ☐ = 1

1 Read the title of each number line. Copy the number
   lines and write in the appropriate fractions or decimals.
   On some lines, not all the scale marks will need a value.

You will need:
- coloured pencils

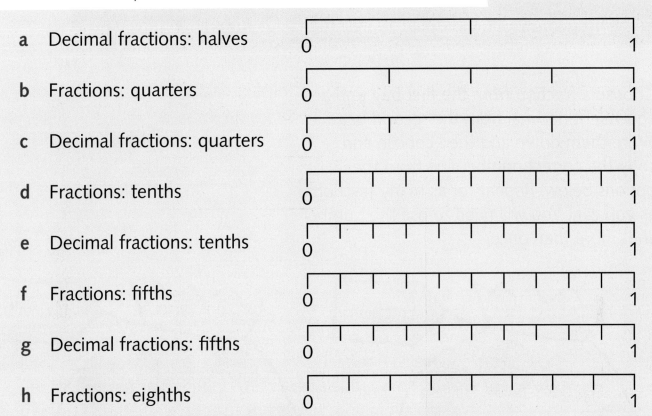

a Decimal fractions: halves

b Fractions: quarters

c Decimal fractions: quarters

d Fractions: tenths

e Decimal fractions: tenths

f Fractions: fifths

g Decimal fractions: fifths

h Fractions: eighths

i Decimal fractions: eighths

2 Look at all your number lines from Question 1. Using coloured
   pencils, circle the fractions and decimals that are equivalent.
   Can you find any groups of three that are equivalent?

1 Explain clearly why $\frac{1}{8} = 0.125$. Read your explanation to a partner. Ask them
   to give you some feedback about how well you have explained the maths.

2 What decimal is equivalent to each of the fractions below? Explain to a partner
   how you worked them out.

$\frac{1}{20}$ $\frac{5}{20}$ $\frac{13}{20}$ $\frac{15}{20}$ $\frac{19}{20}$

3 What do you notice about the decimal equivalents for
   these two fractions? Why is this?

$\frac{1}{3}$ $\frac{2}{3}$

Fraction and decimal equivalents (2)

Associate a fraction with division and calculate decimal fraction equivalents

 Challenge 1

Choose a fraction from the first bag and an equivalent decimal from the second bag. Write them down and then choose and copy the correct number line from the options below. Repeat for as many fractions as you can. You will need to use the number lines more than once.

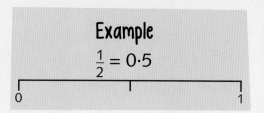

Example

$\frac{1}{2} = 0.5$

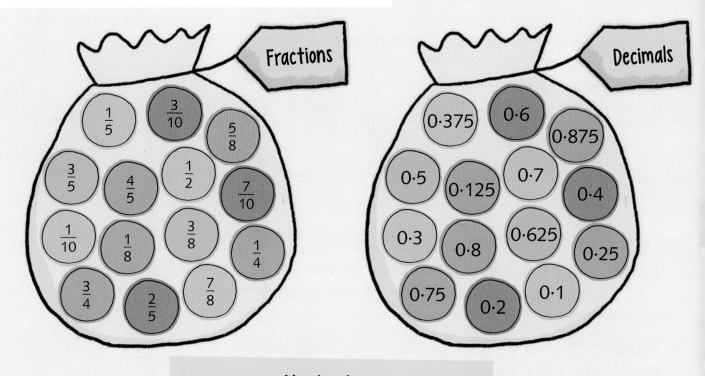

Fractions: $\frac{1}{5}$ $\frac{3}{10}$ $\frac{5}{8}$ $\frac{3}{5}$ $\frac{4}{5}$ $\frac{1}{2}$ $\frac{7}{10}$ $\frac{1}{10}$ $\frac{1}{8}$ $\frac{3}{8}$ $\frac{1}{4}$ $\frac{3}{4}$ $\frac{2}{5}$ $\frac{7}{8}$

Decimals: 0.375 0.6 0.875 0.5 0.125 0.7 0.4 0.3 0.8 0.625 0.25 0.75 0.2 0.1

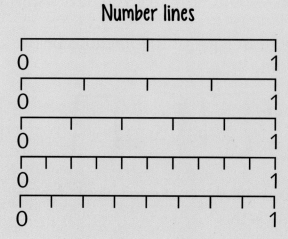

Number lines

1 For each fraction, write a calculation to find its decimal equivalent and then work it out. Check your answers using a calculator.

You will need:
• calculator

a $\frac{1}{2}$　　b $\frac{1}{4}$　　c $\frac{3}{4}$　　d $\frac{1}{5}$　　e $\frac{3}{10}$

f $\frac{7}{10}$　　g $\frac{2}{5}$　　h $\frac{3}{8}$　　i $\frac{4}{5}$　　j $\frac{4}{10}$

> **Example**
> $\frac{1}{2} = 1 \div 2 = 0.5$

2 Write these fractions in two groups under the headings 'Less than half' and 'More than half'.

$\frac{3}{9}$　$\frac{7}{12}$　$\frac{2}{7}$　$\frac{1}{3}$　$\frac{4}{7}$　$\frac{2}{11}$　$\frac{5}{12}$　$\frac{8}{9}$　$\frac{6}{15}$　$\frac{8}{13}$　$\frac{2}{3}$　$\frac{6}{7}$

3 Change each fraction in Question 2 to a decimal to check if you were correct.

4 Explain why the numerator divided by the denominator in a fraction is the way to find the decimal equivalent.

> I can check that $\frac{7}{9}$ is more than half as the decimal equivalent is 0·77777778 and this is higher than 0·5.

1 Work out the decimal equivalent for each fraction. What do you notice about the decimals? Why do ninths make this pattern?

$\frac{1}{9}$　$\frac{2}{9}$　$\frac{3}{9}$　$\frac{4}{9}$　$\frac{5}{9}$　$\frac{6}{9}$　$\frac{7}{9}$　$\frac{8}{9}$

You will need:
• calculator

2 Work out the decimal equivalent for each fraction. Round each one to a decimal number with 3 places.

> **Example**
> $\frac{2}{7} = 2 \div 7 = 0.2857143$
> $\frac{2}{7} = 0.286$

a $\frac{4}{7}$　　b $\frac{6}{13}$　　c $\frac{3}{14}$　　d $\frac{7}{12}$

e $\frac{9}{11}$　　f $\frac{1}{17}$　　g $\frac{2}{3}$　　h $\frac{6}{7}$

> As the 7 in my decimal equivalent is larger than 5, I have to round the thousandths digit up to 6. So $\frac{2}{7}$ to 3 decimal places is 0·286.

Fractions, decimals and percentages (1)

Recall and use equivalences between fractions, decimals and percentages

Challenge 1

1 Write the fraction and the decimal that are equivalent to each percentage.

Example

$$13\% = \frac{13}{100} = 0 \cdot 13$$

Remember they are all hundredths.

a 1%   b 25%   c 7%   d 24%   e 36%

f 41%   g 55%   h 63%   i 79%   j 86%

k 92%   l 99%   m 11%   n 19%   o 48%

p 57%   q 68%   r 5%   s 37%   t 71%

2 Why do fractions, decimals and percentages all go together?

Challenge 2

1 Work out the decimal equivalent and two fraction equivalents for each percentage.

a 25%   b 80%   c 50%   d 30%   e 75%

f 40%   g 20%   h 60%   i 10%   j 90%

2 Write the percentage, fraction and decimal equivalents that are hidden in the clouds.

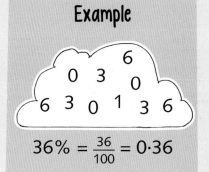
a

b
0 1   2
2 5 0

c

d
7 5 0
5 3 7 4

e
            9
   0 2 0
9 2 0 1 2 9

f
0 1   1
0 1 1 0

g
      2
4   0
   1
5 2   5

h
0   6 5
   6   1 0
5 0   6 5

i
      6
0   3
5 0   6

j
      1
0 1   0
1 3 0 1 3 3

k
         2
0 2   0
   2   1
2 0   2 2

---

1 Work out the decimal and simplified fraction equivalent for each percentage.

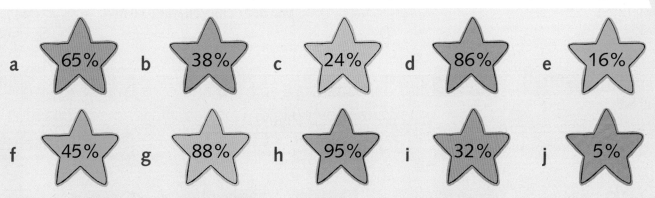

a 65%   b 38%   c 24%   d 86%   e 16%

f 45%   g 88%   h 95%   i 32%   j 5%

---

2 Many people refer to one third as 33% and two thirds as 66%. Is this mathematically correct? Explain your answer.

Calculating percentages

Solve problems involving the calculation of percentages and the use of percentages for comparison

Challenge 1

1 Work out these percentages.

a 50% of 1600	**b** 50% of 3000	**c** 25% of 4000
d 10% of 3800	**e** 10% of 5100	**f** 30% of 6200
g 40% of 5300	**h** 70% of 7100	**i** 50% of 1400

2 Use the information in the yellow box to answer the questions.

> • 1200 people went to a show.
> • Ticket sales raised: €3400.
> • Programme sales raised: €2800.

a 25% of the total money raised was given to charity. How much money was given to charity?

b 40% of the audience were children. How many children were there?

c 12% of people arrived by bus, 27% arrived by car, 36% walked and the rest came by train. What percentage of people came by train? How many people came by train?

Challenge 2

1 Work out each of the percentages of the amounts in the middle for each question.

> Remember, one way to work out the answer is to find 1% and multiply the result by the per cent you want to find.

a
30%	25%
7800	
18%	80%

b
23%	75%
8100	
49%	60%

c
61%	40%
9300	
5%	79%

d
46%	20%
8800	
65%	11%

e
90%	36%
9700	
53%	3%

f
13%	20%
12 500	
75%	99%

2 What is an efficient way to work out 99%?

3 Use the information in the yellow box to answer the questions.

> - 6400 people went to a concert.
> - Ticket sales raised: €9800.
> - Ice-cream sales raised: €2800.

a 45% of the ticket sales was used to pay the band. How much money was that?

b Of the people who bought ice creams, 35% bought strawberry, 44% bought chocolate and the rest bought vanilla. How much money was raised from the sale of vanilla ice creams?

c 800 programmes were sold throughout the evening. Halfway through the evening, 70% of the programmes had been sold at 80c each. The price of the remaining programmes was reduced by 10% and they were all sold. What was the total amount of money raised by selling programmes?

d At the end of the concert, 5% of people drove home, 25% caught a bus, 42% walked and the rest caught a train. How many travelled by each mode of transport?

1 Work out each of the percentages of the amounts in the middle for each question. Some of your answers will be decimals.

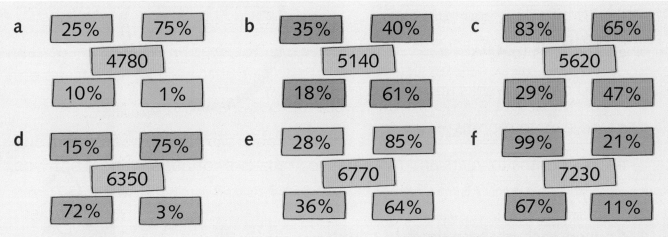

a
| 25% | 75% |
| 4780 |
| 10% | 1% |

b
| 35% | 40% |
| 5140 |
| 18% | 61% |

c
| 83% | 65% |
| 5620 |
| 29% | 47% |

d
| 15% | 75% |
| 6350 |
| 72% | 3% |

e
| 28% | 85% |
| 6770 |
| 36% | 64% |

f
| 99% | 21% |
| 7230 |
| 67% | 11% |

2 The information in the yellow box describes how the money raised for a charity concert was spent. Use the information to answer the questions.

> - 5% was spent on printing the programmes.
> - 36% was used to pay the band.
> - 10% was used to pay the staff.
> - 24% was given to charity.
> - There was €2450 left.

a How much money was raised altogether?

b How was the money divided between each item?

Converting units of time

Convert from smaller to larger units of time and vice versa

Challenge 1

1 Convert each of these times to minutes.

   a 1 h 40 min   **b** 2 h 20 min   **c** 4 h 30 min   **d** 3 h 16 min

2 Convert each of these times to hours and minutes.

   a 90 min   **b** 160 min   **c** 200 min   **d** 165 min

3 Convert these times to the units given.

   a 95 s to minutes and seconds

   b 2 min 40 s to seconds

   c 3 days to hours

   d 50 h to days and hours

   e 4 weeks to days

   f 40 days to weeks and days

   g 6 years to months

   h 50 months to years and months

Challenge 2

1 Convert each of these times to minutes.

   a 3 h 25 min   **b** 5 h 42 min   **c** 10 h 37 min

   d 12 h 14 min   **e** 1 day   **f** 1 week

2 Convert each of these times to hours and minutes.

   a 250 min   **b** 400 min   **c** 505 min   **d** 1000 min

3 Convert these times to the units given.

  a 144 s to minutes and seconds

  b 9 min 48 s to seconds

  c 7 days to hours

  d 75 h to days and hours

  e 13 weeks to days

  f 130 days to weeks and days

  g 8 years to months

  h 80 months to years and months

  i 10 years to weeks

  j 100 weeks to years and weeks

4 How many:

  a seconds in 1 hour?

  b minutes in 1 day?

  c hours in 1 week?

5 If your heart beats once every second, how many times will it beat in a day?

1 Copy and complete the table.

Hours (h)	0·1	0·2	0·3	0·4	0·5
Minutes (min)	6				

2 Convert each of these times to hours and minutes.

  a 3·4 h   **b** 2·7 h   **c** 5·8 h   **d** 3·6 h

3 Convert these times to hours using decimals.

  a 2 h 18 min   **b** 7 h 42 min   **c** 9 h 54 min   **d** 12 h 12 min

4 How long is:

  a 1 million seconds in completed days?

  b 1 million minutes in completed weeks?

  c 1 million hours in completed years?

Problems involving time

Calculate and convert between units of time to solve problems

Challenge 1

Use the table to answer these questions.

Swimming pool opening hours		
Day	Opening time	Closing time
Sun	10:00 a.m.	5:00 p.m.
Mon–Fri	7:30 a.m.	9:00 p.m.
Sat	9:00 a.m.	6:00 p.m.

1 On which day or days is the pool open for nine hours?

2 For how many hours is the pool open on a Wednesday?

3 On Sunday, Garry arrived at the leisure centre at 9:47 a.m. How many minutes did he have to wait until the swimming pool opened?

4 On Friday, Helen left the swimming pool at 20:23. How many minutes after she left did the pool close?

5 Iain swims for 45 minutes every day except Sunday. How much time, in hours and minutes, does he spend in the pool each week?

Challenge 2

1 The leisure centre is holding a swimming event to raise money for charity.

a Year 6 enters a team of eight swimmers in the relay event. Each swimmer, in turn, completes 4 lengths of the pool in an average time of 50 seconds per length. How many minutes and seconds does the team take to complete their swim?

b Melissa completed 4 lengths of the pool in 3 minutes and 40 seconds. If she continued to swim at this rate, how long would it take her to complete 20 lengths of the pool?

c Nico swam 24 lengths of the pool in 19 minutes. If he completed his swim at 11:07 a.m., at what time did he begin his first length of the pool?

2   There are exactly 6 weeks to the end of the school term.
    After 10 days, how many days will there be until the end of term?

3   On your 12th birthday, how many weeks old are you?

4   At Bert's Bakery, Bert makes apple pies and custard pies.

•   The apple pies are baked for 25 minutes and the
    custard pies are baked for 20 minutes.

•   As each tray of pies is finished, it is taken from the
    oven and a new tray is put in.

•   At 11:15 a.m. Bert puts one tray of apple pies and
    one tray of custard pies into the oven.

When is the next time that Bert puts a tray of apple pies
and a tray of custard pies into the oven at the same time?

5   One day on planet Earth lasts 24 hours.
    Tom spends one quarter of each day at school.
    Calculate the number of hours and minutes
    Tom would spend at school each day if he lived
    on each of these planets and spent one quarter
    of his day at school.

Planet	Mercury	Venus	Earth	Mars	Jupiter	Uranus	Pluto*
Hours in 1 day	59	243	24	25	10	17	153

*Pluto is a dwarf planet

Using the table in Question 5 of Challenge 2,
calculate the number of hours and minutes
you would spend asleep on each of the
planets each day if you slept for the same
fraction of time as you do on Earth.

Finding the average speed

Calculate speed using compound units

Challenges 1, 2

1 Work out each speed.

a 40 km in 1 hour   b 25 miles in 1 hour

c 5 km in 1 hour   d 62 km in 1 hour

e 500 miles in 1 hour   f 14 km in 1 hour

> **Example**
> 30 km in 1 hour = 30 km/h
> 20 miles in 1 hour = 20 mph

2 Find the average speed of each motorcyclist in kilometres per hour.

> **Example**
> 90 km in 3 hours
> Speed = 90 ÷ 3
> = 30 km/h

a

100 km in 2 hours

b

160 km in 4 hours

c

240 km in 6 hours

d

150 km in 5 hours

e

105 km in 3 hours

Challenge 2

1 Find the average speed of each lorry in miles per hour.

a

120 miles in 4 hours

b

225 miles in 5 hours

c

210 miles in 6 hours

2 Calculate the average speed of each vehicle in kilometres per hour.

a  b

> **Example**
> 12 km in $\frac{1}{2}$ hour
> 24 km in 1 hour
> Speed = 24 km/h

20 km in $\frac{1}{4}$ hour   15 km in $\frac{1}{2}$ hour

c  d  e

7·5 km in $\frac{1}{2}$ hour   2·5 km in $\frac{1}{3}$ hour   1·2 km in $\frac{1}{5}$ hour

3 Double each distance in Question 2 and write the new speed.

4 The speed limit for a lorry is 100 km/h. If the driver travels 360 kilometres in 4 hours, how does the actual average speed compare to its speed limit?

1 A long-distance lorry driver travels on the motorway at an average speed of 80 kilometres per hour. Copy and complete the table.

Time (h)	$\frac{1}{4}$	$\frac{1}{2}$	1	2	3	4
Distance (km)			80			

2 A container ship crosses the North Sea at an average speed of 18 kilometres per hour. Copy and complete the table.

Time (h)			1			
Distance (km)	4·5	9	18	36	54	72

Calculating speed

Calculate speed using compound units

Challenge 1

1 Write each speed using the correct unit of speed in each answer.

    a 17 m in 1 second   **b** 30 cm in 1 minute

    c 900 m in 1 hour   **d** 7 cm in 1 second

> **Example**
>
> 50 cm in 1 minute
> Speed = 50 cm/min

2 Work out the average speed of each of the following:

    a swallow: 3500 m in 7 minutes

    b tortoise: 300 cm in 15 minutes

    c sheep: 360 m in 30 minutes

    d snail: 3·9 cm in 3 seconds

    e grizzly bear: 330 m in 5 minutes

    f cheetah: 3·2 km in 2 minutes

> **Example**
>
> 45 cm in 5 minutes
> Speed = 9 cm/min

Challenge 2

1 Three children were timed swimming.

    • Matt swam 500 m in 4 minutes.

    • Leon swam 450 m in 5 minutes.

    • Ken swam 600 m in 6 minutes.

    a Find the average speed of each swimmer in metres per minute.

    b List the swimmers in order, from fastest to slowest.

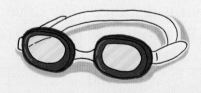

2 Calculate each average speed in metres per hour and then in kilometres per hour.

    a 800 m in 30 minutes   **b** 500 m in 15 minutes

    c 250 m in 10 minutes   **d** 350 m in 20 minutes

    e 1300 m in 15 minutes   **f** 740 m in 6 minutes

> **Example**
>
> 420 m in 15 minutes
> (420 m × 4) in 1 hour
> Speed = 1680 m/h
> = 1·68 km/h

3 Three aeroplanes flew the following distances:

- Aeroplane A flew 2268 miles in 4 hours.

- Aeroplane B flew 2735 miles in 5 hours.

- Aeroplane C flew 3180 miles in 6 hours.

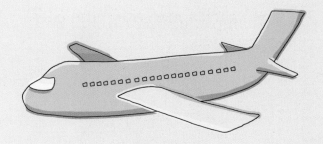

a Find the average speed of each aircraft in miles per hour (mph).

b If Aeroplane A flew for 6 hours at the same average speed, how many more miles would it have travelled than Aeroplane C?

4 A glacier in the French Alps moved 168 cm in one week. What was its average speed in centimetres per day?

5 In 2012, the Jakobshavn Glacier in Greenland was recorded as moving at about 40 metres per day. If the glacier had continued to move at this speed, what would its speed have been in kilometres per year?

1 Light travels at approximately 300 000 kilometres per second.

a How many kilometres will light travel in 5 seconds?

b The Earth is 150 million kilometres from the Sun. Find how long it takes the light from the Sun to travel to Earth in:

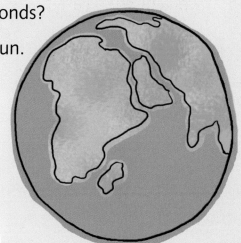

    i   seconds
    ii minutes to one decimal place

2 Mercury is 91 million kilometres from the Sun. How many minutes, to the nearest minute, will it take the light from the Sun to reach Mercury?

Maths facts

Addition and subtraction

Whole numbers

Example: 456 287 + 359 849

```
    456 287
  + 359 849
    816 136
    1 1 1  1 1
```

Example: 746 291 − 298 354

```
    6 13 15 12 8 11
    7̶4̶6̶ 2̶9̶1̶
  − 298 354
    447 937
```

Decimals

Example: 57·486 + 45·378

```
    57·486
  + 45·378
   102·864
    1    1 1
```

Example: 63·237 − 45·869

```
    5 12  11 12 17
    6̶3̶·2̶3̶7̶
  − 45·869
    17·368
```

Multiplication and division

Written methods – short multiplication

Whole numbers

Example: 5643 × 8

Formal written method

```
      5643
  ×   5 3 2 8
     45144
```

Decimals

Example: 4·83 × 6

Partitioning

4·83 × 6 = (4 × 6) + (0·8 × 6) + (0·03 × 6)
      = 24 + 4·8 + 0·18
      = 28·98

Grid method

×	4	0·8	0·03
6	24	4·8	0·18	= 28·98

Expanded written method

4·83 × 6 is equivalent to 483 × 6 ÷ 100

```
      483
  ×     6
       18  (   3 × 6)
      480  (  80 × 6)
     2400  ( 400 × 6)
     2898
```

2898 ÷ 100 = 28·98

Formal written method

```
      483
  ×  4 1 6
     2898
```

2898 ÷ 100 = 28·98

Written methods – long multiplication
Whole numbers

Example: 285 × 63

Partitioning

285 × 63 = (200 × 63) + (80 × 63) + (5 × 63)
= 12 600 + 5040 + 315
= 17 955

Grid method

×	200	80	5
60	12 000	4800	300
3	600	240	15

17 100
+   855
17 955

Expanded written method

```
    2 8 5              or        2 8 5
 ×    6 3                     ×    6 3
 1 7⁵1³0 0  (285 × 60)          8⁵5²1 5  (285 ×  3)
   8⁵5²1 5  (285 ×  3)       1 7⁵1³0 0  (285 × 60)
 1 7 9 5 5                   1 7 9 5 5
```

Formal written method

```
    2 8 5
 ×    6 3
   8⁵5²1 5
 1 7⁵1³0 0
 1 7 9 5 5
```

Decimals

Example: 7·56 × 34

Partitioning

7·56 × 34 = (7 × 34) + (0·5 × 34) + (0·06 × 34)
= 238 + 17 + 2·04
= 257·04

Grid method

×	7	0·5	0·06
30	210	15	1·8
4	28	2	0·24

226·80
+ 30·24
257·04
   1

Expanded written method

7·56 × 34 is equivalent to 756 × 34 ÷ 100

```
    7 5 6           or        7 5 6
 ×    3 4                  ×    3 4
 2 2⁶1 8 0 (756 × 30)       3 0²2⁴ (756 ×  4)
   3 0²2⁴ (756 ×  4)      2 2⁶1 8 0 (756 × 30)
 2 5 7 0 4                 2 5 7 0 4
         1                         1
```

25 704 ÷ 100 = 257·04   25 704 ÷ 100 = 257·04

Formal written method

7·56 × 34 is equivalent to 756 × 34 ÷ 100

```
    7 5 6
 ×    3 4
   3 0²2⁴
 2 2⁶1 8 0
 2 5 7 0 4
         1
```

25 704 ÷ 100 = 257·04

Written methods – short division
Whole numbers

Example: 1838 ÷ 8

Whole number remainder

```
    2 2 9 r 6
 8)1 8 ²3 ⁷8
```

Fraction remainder

```
    2 2 9 ¾
 8)1 8 ²3 ⁷8
```

Decimal remainder

```
    2 2 9 · 7 5
 8)1 8 ²3 ⁷8 · ⁶0 ⁴0
```

Decimals

Example: 45·36 ÷ 6

45·36 ÷ 6 is equivalent to 4536 ÷ 6 ÷ 100

```
     7 · 5 6                      7 5 6
6 ) 4 5 ·³3 ³6     or       6 ) 4 5³3 ³6
```
$$756 \div 100 = 7·56$$

Written methods – long division
Whole numbers

Example: 5836 ÷ 18

Expanded written method

```
        3 2 4 r 4
18 ) 5 8 3 6
   − 5 4 0 0      (300 × 18)
      ³ ¹³
       4 3 6
   −     3 6 0    ( 20 × 18)
           7 6
   −       7 2    (  4 × 18)
             4
```

$$5836 \div 18 = 324 \text{ r } 4 \quad \text{or} \quad 324\tfrac{2}{9}$$

Formal written method

```
        3 2 4 r 4
18 ) 5 8 3 6
   − 5 4 ↓ ↓
        4 3
   −    3 6
          7 6
   −      7 2
            4
```

$$5836 \div 18 = 324 \text{ r } 4 \quad \text{or} \quad 324\tfrac{2}{9}$$

Decimals

Example: 58·32 ÷ 18

Expanded written method

58·32 ÷ 18 is equivalent to 5832 ÷ 18 ÷ 100

```
        3 2 4
18 ) 5 8 3 2
   − 5 4 0 0      (300 × 18)
      ³ ¹³
       4 3 2
   −     3 6 0    ( 20 × 18)
           7 2
   −       7 2    (  4 × 18)
             0
```
$$324 \div 100 = 3·24$$

or

```
        3 · 2 4
18 ) 5 8 · 3 2
   − 5 4 · 0 0    (  3 × 18)
      ³ ¹³
       4 · 3 2
   −     3 · 6 0  ( 0·2 × 18)
         0 · 7 2
   −     0 · 7 2  (0·04 × 18)
         0 · 0 0
```

Formal written method

58·32 ÷ 18 is equivalent to 5832 ÷ 18 ÷ 100

```
        3 2 4
18 ) 5 8 3 2
   −  5 4 ↓
        4 3
   −    3 6 ↓
          7 2
   −      7 2
           0
```

or

```
         3 · 2 4
18 ) 5 8 · 3 2
   −  5 4 · ↓
        4 · 3
   −    3 · 6 ↓
          0 · 7 2
   −      0 · 7 2
             0
```

324 ÷ 100 = 3·24

Fractions, decimals and percentages

$\frac{1}{100} = 0.01 = 1\%$

$\frac{2}{100} = \frac{1}{50} = 0.02 = 2\%$

$\frac{4}{100} = \frac{1}{25} = 0.04 = 4\%$

$\frac{5}{100} = \frac{1}{20} = 0.05 = 5\%$

$\frac{10}{100} = \frac{1}{10} = 0.1 = 10\%$

$\frac{20}{100} = \frac{1}{5} = 0.2 = 20\%$

$\frac{25}{100} = \frac{1}{4} = 0.25 = 25\%$

$\frac{40}{100} = \frac{2}{5} = 0.4 = 40\%$

$\frac{50}{100} = \frac{1}{2} = 0.5 = 50\%$

$\frac{75}{100} = \frac{3}{4} = 0.75 = 75\%$

$\frac{80}{100} = \frac{4}{5} = 0.8 = 80\%$

$\frac{100}{100} = \frac{10}{10} = 1 = 100\%$

$\frac{2}{5} + \frac{4}{5} = \frac{6}{5}$

$= 1\frac{1}{5}$

$\frac{7}{8} - \frac{3}{8} = \frac{4}{8}$

$= \frac{1}{2}$

$\frac{2}{3} \times 4 = \frac{2}{3} \times \frac{4}{1}$

$= \frac{2 \times 4}{3 \times 1}$

$= \frac{8}{3}$

$= 2\frac{2}{3}$

$2\frac{3}{4} \times 3 = \frac{11}{4} \times 3$

$= \frac{11 \times 3}{4 \times 1}$

$= \frac{33}{4}$

$= 8\frac{1}{4}$

$9\frac{2}{3} + 6\frac{4}{5}$

$9 + 6 = 15$

$\frac{2}{3} + \frac{4}{5} = \frac{10}{15} + \frac{12}{15}$

$= \frac{22}{15}$

$= 1\frac{7}{15}$

$1\frac{7}{15} + 15 = 16\frac{7}{15}$

$11\frac{3}{4} - 7\frac{2}{6}$

$11 - 7 = 4$

$\frac{3}{4} - \frac{2}{6} = \frac{9}{12} - \frac{4}{12}$

$= \frac{5}{12}$

$\frac{5}{12} + 4 = 4\frac{5}{12}$

$\frac{1}{2} \times \frac{3}{4} = \frac{1 \times 3}{2 \times 4}$

$= \frac{3}{8}$

$\frac{2}{3} \div 4 = \frac{2}{3 \times 4}$

$= \frac{2}{12}$

$= \frac{1}{6}$

Measurement

Length

1 km = 1000 m = 100 000 cm

0·1 km = 100 m = 10 000 cm = 100 000 mm

0·01 km = 10 m = 1000 cm = 10 000 mm

1 m = 100 cm = 1000 mm

0·1 m = 10 cm = 100 mm

0·01 m = 1 cm = 10 mm

0·001 m = 0·1 cm = 1 mm

1 cm = 10 mm

0·1 cm = 1 mm

Metric units and imperial units – Length

1 km $\approx \frac{5}{8}$ miles (8 km ≈ 5 miles)

1 inch ≈ 2·5 cm

Perimeter, area and volume

P = perimeter A = area V = volume

l = length w = width b = base h = height

Perimeter of a rectangle

$P = 2(l + w)$

Perimeter of a square

$P = 4 \times l$ or $P = 4l$

Area of a rectangle

$A = l \times w$ or $A = lw$

Area of a triangle

$A = \frac{1}{2} \times b \times h$ or $A = \frac{1}{2}bh$

Area of a parallelogram

$A = b \times h$ or $A = bh$

Volume of a cuboid

$V = l \times w \times h$ or $V = lwh$

Capacity

1 litre = 1000 ml

0·1 l = 100 ml

0·01 l = 10 ml

0·001 l = 1 ml

1 cl = 10 ml

24-hour time

Mass

1 t = 1000 kg   1 kg = 1000 g   0·1 kg = 100 g   0·01 kg = 10 g   0·001 kg = 1 g

Geometry

Parts of a circle

circumference

centre

radius

diameter

Coordinates

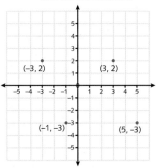

(−3, 2)   (3, 2)

(−1, −3)   (5, −3)

Translation

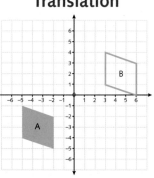

Shape A has been translated 8 squares to the right and 5 squares up.

Reflection

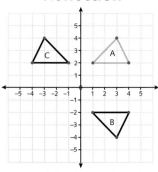

Shape A has been reflected in the x-axis (Shape B) and in the y-axis (Shape C).